Coming To Terms

Coming To Terms

A Collection Of Essays

H. Palmer Hall

Plain View Press
P. O. 42255
Austin, TX 78704

plainviewpress.net
sb@plainviewpress.net
1-512-441-2452

ISBN: 978-1-891386-89-3
Library of Congress Number: 9781891386893

Cover art and photos by H. Palmer Hall.

Acknowledgments

The author would like to thank the editors of the following literary reviews in which these essays first appeared:

Ascent: "An Introduction of Sorts," originally published as "Thinking About Poetry"; *Concho River Review*: "Dixie Hotel Aubade"; *From the Periphery: poems and essays*: "Basic Training"; *Gruene Street Review*: "Driving Somewhere"; *In a Field of Flowers* (MacMillan anthology): "Coming to Terms with Dad"; *New Texas*: "Dancing in the Thicket"; *Palo Alto Review*: "Snapshots on the Road to Peace" (A section of "Snapshots" first appeared in *The Texas Writers' Newsletter* as "Poetry in Viet-Nam") and "The Big Thicket and the Death of James Byrd, Jr."; *Pecan Grove Review*: "It Takes a Family" and "Coming to Terms"; *The Practice of Peace*: "Father Buddha" (reprinted in *War, Literature & the Arts*); *RiverSedge*: "Places to Grow" (included in *Best Texas Writing II*); *Salt River Review* "A True Story About an Old Woman and Poetry" (later republished in the *Atlanta Hospice Association Newsletter*); *Small Press Review*: "A Hell of a Job" and "On Rejection and Acceptance, All Wrapped Up With The Beats"; *Tattoo Highway*: "Driving Through Milwaukee"; *Texas Review*: "Studying Languages in Graduate School" (An earlier version was published in *Eclectica* as "The Woman of My German Summer"); *Valparaiso Poetry Review*: "Why I Still Write about the War"; *VietNam Generation*: "A Brief Stay in Chu Lai".

Contents

An Introduction of Sorts
Thinking About Poetry

It is fairly late at night and I am writing again for the first time in several weeks and I am thinking about poetry. I am thinking, too, about the year I was seven years old and my doctor told me I was going blind in my right eye. Yes, I am thinking about that, but I am thinking mostly about poetry and only a little about surgical "procedures" and about how everything these days is a "process." Everything, including poetry and the surgery that repaired my right eye, is movement toward something or, perhaps, away from something else.

I am thinking about poetry and I am afraid I am boring you, but it is getting very late at night and I am thinking about my medical examination this morning, and about the nurse who connected a dozen tapes to my chest and side and about her long red fingernails pressing down on the membrane that keyed instructions into the EKG. I did not watch the squiggle marks on the paper feeding out of the machine, but the sharp gleam of the nail polish and how she typed with the points of her nails.

When the doctor called later to tell me my heart was fine and my blood pressure was normal and my cholesterol was where it belonged and my prostate seemed normal and even my gall bladder (suspect organ) didn't have to join my right kidney in that place where body parts go when they are harmful and have to be ripped out, I thought then about poetry and about the process of semi-annual medical examinations that do not search for something, but for nothing, and about bright red fingernails.

To walk across the street is a dangerous thing, I thought, and to write a poem can also be dangerous. Writing the best poems must, I suspect, always be dangerous, as dangerous, at least, as crossing a street with our eyes closed. When I was seven years old and my doctor told me that I was going blind in my right eye, I went with my family to my grandmother's house in northern Florida. We drove from Southeast Texas as we did every summer and turned off Highway 98 onto a sand road that meandered through a wilderness until it stopped at a small bay off a larger bay. I did not think about poetry then, but the place was poetry and the place was dangerous.

The first morning I was there, I pushed a small wooden boat off the shore at Wakulla Beach and lay down in it, feeling my body rock with the low waves, and let the boat drift away from shore, my eyes closed in the hot sun. From time to time, I would open only my left eye and stare up at the clouds and wonder what it would be like to be blind in one eye, no longer to have depth perception. The boat drifted out of Wakulla Bay and into Appalachee Bay and by the time I sat up, and took the oars in my hands, I had no idea of where on that body of water I was.

At seven years old, alone in an old 12-foot, wooden boat, I dipped the oars into the water and stroked aimlessly in what might have been the direction of shore. Poetry is like this for me much of the time. I am alone in a large body of water and I put the oars in the locks and pull the water past me. It travels under the boat, the boat does not really move. For a poem to be good, to be worth writing, for me at least, it has to be like that and it does not matter where it comes from.

I am staying up very late tonight and I am thinking about poetry and I am thinking about myself when I was a small boy and was told that I was going blind. Poetry is dangerous, I think, if it is poetry worth doing. Poetry is risk taking, pushing yourself and your words out there into water so deep that a single wave can drown you.

I remember when that small boat drifted farther and farther out and I finally sat up and looked around and could not see land in any direction, only a faint smudge back in the direction I must have drifted from, I simply did not care. Someone would have found me after more time had passed, but I was lucky and the tide turned, washing in towards East Goose Creek and Wakulla Bay.

It is late and I am writing tonight for the first time in many weeks and I am thinking about those first moments when, as a young boy, I dipped the blades of my oars into silvery water and pulled the water under the boat, turning toward shore. That moment was poetry, that single moment of awareness, and though I did not write a poem that day, nor any day after that for many years, that day was itself a poem.

So, tonight, I am thinking about me when I was seven years old and about turning fifty-three on Sunday and about poetry and danger and surgery and blinded eyes and kidneys thrown into biomedical waste containers, but mostly I am thinking about poetry.

It Takes a Family

I have been reading Terry Tempest Williams' "The Village Watchman," a fine tribute to her Uncle Allen, who was born with oxygen deprivation and spent many years institutionalized. It's a fine essay, well worth reading, and reminded me of my Aunt Clifton. Clifton Hall was one of my father's five sisters, most of whom lived out their lives on the beach at Wakulla Bay some miles south of Tallahassee in what is now the St. Marks Wildlife Refuge. My grandmother had no problems with Clifton's birth, but at six years old that youngest of her five daughters and five sons contracted scarlet fever and remained, mentally, at that age until her death at age 86.

She was a fixture of our visits to my grandmother's old house every summer and would wade with us through the tidal flats and estuaries made by East Goose Creek to search for blue crabs or just to wander in the clear salt water and look at sting rays, sea horses, star fish and occasional horseshoe crabs and minnows. We would take turns pulling the dark green wooden boat along the bay's shore through sea weed and around oyster bars. Clifton would sit in the boat when we had to swim out into the bay to get to one of the shell bars and would hold the croaker sacks open as we emptied the crab nets after successful scoops.

Frequently, she would go with us down to the flats at low tide to round up hundreds of fiddler crabs for bait for the older people—my grandmother, my father and the others who would fish all afternoon and late into the evenings and who would use them as bait for red fish and speckled trout. To get a good supply of fiddler crabs, we would go down to the flats at low tide where you could see them in the hundreds and chase after them, herding them like cowboys rounding up cattle, until they formed a single pile of trembling shell, giant pincher claws waving in the air. When we had them in a tight enough cluster, Clifton would hold a bucket out and we would reach down and pick up handfuls of them and dump them in.

Back at my grandmother's house a hundred yards or so up from the shore, we played countless games of Fish and Battle or stacked dominoes into towers with her. She sat quietly and watched when we played canasta with our cousin Alice Faye and if we stopped to read or rest, she would take a fly swatter and walk around the screened-in porch killing dirt daubers that managed to get in when we left the screen door open.

When my grandmother fell and shattered her hip at age 77, my Aunt Effie moved back into the house and cared for both her and Clifton. It was a primitive house with electricity from a generator and enough power to light only a couple of lamps. Such fresh water as there was we hauled in each week; the well could be trusted for washing salt water from our bodies, but not for drinking. The only heat in the house in winter came from the fireplaces in each bedroom. Until I was well into my teens, we had to chop wood for the stove and for the fireplaces and we used an outhouse for a bathroom.

My grandmother finally died at age 96, nineteen years bedridden, and my Aunt Effie took over the care of her younger sister. When Clifton died, the house was sold and my Aunt moved to Fort Pierce to live with her own daughter. I still own property there on the beach and, some day, hope to build my own house, one of the few that can legally go up on that part of the St. Marks National Wildlife Refuge.

But I have not visited that stretch of beach in several years and, when I do make that trip again, it will not be the same. So much will have changed. My father, his father and his father's father grew up there in that same house that was so weathered by the constant wind that blew in from the bay. But to me, it was always a woman's house—my grandmother's, my aunt's and Clifton's. When I grew older and went fishing with my father, the first sign of civilization we could see from out in the bay was the green roof of my grandmother's house. The first person to rush out and greet us was always Clifton.

The house has undoubtedly been modernized, people who do not know about my grandmother or about Clifton, must live there now. But when I do go back, what I will see in my mind's eye is a six-year-old girl in the body of an 80-year-old woman. She'll wave and run for the cards or for the crab nets or will sit quietly in an old wooden boat while my brother and I pull her along the shore.

Growing up in Southeast Texas

I grew up in Southeast Texas surrounded by some of the loveliest thicket anyone could imagine, though the federal government didn't recognize its nature until long after I had moved away and Senator Ralph Yarborough had finally convinced congress to create the Big Thicket National Preserve.

It was not the Big Thicket, though, that made me grow to appreciate quiet places with dense growths of trees and shrubs. Across from the federal housing project where I lived with my family for a few years stood Junker Woods, an oasis of thicket that separated my home from the school I would walk to each day.

Mornings and afternoons, during the week, I would go barefoot down narrow trails to get to and from the elementary school. Both the school and the woods have vanished in the intervening years, but I had wonderful times there, almost like Robert Frost's New England boys who had been swinging birches. My friends and I would also swing trees, climbing to the tops of young elms and maples until our weight would cause them to bend and gently swing us down to the ground. Then we would let them go, with rocks nestled in the topmost boughs, and laugh as that impromptu ammunition flew off into the woods.

Junker Woods, its trees, trails and small pond, all spoke to me in important ways as I grew up, perhaps because my family was so poor that my brother, sister and I had to construct our own ways of finding value and pleasure outside the old barracks that had been converted into federal housing. Today, the segregated projects where I grew up have been urban renewed, mostly, I suspect, because it is no longer legal to separate black from white families in housing, and Junker Woods has been torn down and replaced with an urban nightmare: a few blocks of cheap housing and dirty stores.

An overwhelming sense of the transient no longer allows me to think of any place as permanently either sacred or profane. When I drive down Gulf Street in Beaumont, Texas, now, deep memories of those woods and of the games we played in them continue to surface, even though I can now see a kind of sickness beneath it all.

We would, for example, play cowboys and Indians and hide in the woods, waiting for the day's enemy to come down one of the trails and fire arrows at them or shout BANG. The white kids normally got to be the Indians and the black kids, from their own housing units, were most often the cowboys. Even then, the romantic idea of the American Indian was big. And we would play Tarzan and swing on thick, wild grape vines from tree to tree, but the black kids didn't much want to play Tarzan games. I didn't realize why until I was much older.

In the late 40s and early 50s, those societal undercurrents, the basic racism that would see me play with African American kids and then go home to ignore them, feeling no sense of economic solidarity, remained deeply buried in all of us, not to bubble to the top of our consciousness until the late 1950s and the 1960s when we heard about Little Rock and Central High School or listened to Dr. King.

It seemed natural in 1953 for me to walk through the woods to school while my friend down the street got on a school bus to be taken across town to the school for African American kids. When buses just like those were used later to take white kids to other schools throughout the country, not just in the South, the howls of protest seemed disingenuous at best. But that was still in the future.

When we were kids out in Junker Woods, we packed together and played together, blacks on one team, whites on the other, almost acting out the demonstrations and riots that would occur later, with little thought of anything except escaping from places like the projects.

A Hell Of a Job

I have done some rather shitty jobs in my time. I don't mean morally shitty, not even the job I did in Vietnam. Just shitty. But perhaps in some way they were all morally objectionable in their exploitation of others.

I was among that legion of young teens back in the late fifties who went out in paneled trucks and were dropped off in middle-class neighborhoods to sell magazines. You know the spiel: "If I sell enough subscriptions I win a free scholarship to college. I'd appreciate your help." You still hear knocks on the door these days with some kid saying the same thing or some variant of it. I'm usually nice to them, but do not subscribe to their magazines or buy their candies. The scam is not perpetrated by the kids but by the supervisors who know the people actually doing the work will wind up with next to nothing for it.

It's been so many years since those days, but I can still picture the old van: a black paneled Ford, dirty, dented up. The supervisor was maybe 25 and there were four of us cooped up in the back. No air conditioning, the temperature in the high 90s along with the humidity. We boys were all white. This was Southeast Texas and Brown vs. the Board of Education hasn't happened yet though I cannot think of why anyone would want to be equal-opportunitied into this job though I know many would have. We were all happy when the van stopped and we could spill out into the streets, get a taste of fresh air and cool off under a tree.

After the Ford left, we began to walk. What can I say about walking up to the doors and knocking, about people who just took a quick look and then slammed the door, about others who yelled "Fuck you!" before slamming the door, about the too rare victories when someone actually did subscribe to *Ladies Home Journal* or *Field and Stream* or some other magazine? I was thirteen years old and for each magazine I sold I received a very small commission, maybe ten cents, certainly not much more. When the van returned to pick us up late in the afternoon, we had quotas we had to have met. I do not remember the exact quota, only that you lost your job if you failed to meet your quota for two days out of any week. The really sad thing was that there were so many boys waiting for those jobs if one us didn't sell enough subscriptions.

I was good at the whole business. To start with, I was rather small for my age and probably looked closer to ten than thirteen. I was slender with a mop of sun-bleached, blondish hair and walked barefoot from house to house. None of that was intentional, not a sales gimmick. And, what the hell, the housewife of the fifties liked me. So, I always made my quota and more. I easily earned as much as three dollars a day.

So many years later, I can see that I was a victim of exploitation, more so than those women I exploited, and I wonder about that. Who was the exploiter? *Ladies' Home Journal*? *Field and Stream*? The hundred or so magazines that benefited from the hordes of small boys making maybe fifteen to twenty cents an hour if they were lucky? Or was it Troy, the guy who drove the black Ford truck? Or Troy's boss? I think about this off and on, not obsessively, no, but out of mild curiosity. You see, that was my first job in the publishing business (do insert a forced grin here) and the publishing business as a business probably is as shitty as any business. Oh, sure, throw a little glamour in. It looks great to have an article, story or poem in *The New Yorker*, *The Atlantic*, *Esquire*, *Good Housekeeping*. I sold all those magazines, door to door, back in the late fifties when I was thirteen years old.

I think this whole thing came back to me because I got one of those knocks on the door only yesterday. Young, maybe 16, black and muscular, he rang the doorbell. He was working to earn a scholarship to college and wanted me to subscribe to 3 or 4 magazines, just to help him out. I didn't, but I did tell him that I had done the same work when I was even younger than he was. I suggested that he might make more money by mowing lawns or delivering newspapers. He told me to fuck off and walked next door to my neighbors' house.

It hasn't stopped—this exploitation of young people by the publishing industry. I can hear the editors, the publishers, even the writers if I were to publish something like this. "It's not us; it's the magazine agents. It's unscrupulous other people who are doing this. Our job is to put out a good magazine." And, of course, they have other marketing venues. Publishers' Clearinghouse, for example. At least they're not exploiting children, only people who subscribe to magazines as if they were playing the lottery.

If you go right down to the bottom rung of it all, the magazine industry is a pretty shitty business. Those of us who publish in little literary magazines rarely get paid for our magazine contributions (we get contributors' copies) and the small magazines we publish in are not part of this scam, but we'd like to be in magazines that are: *The New Yorker, Esquire's* special fiction issues, *The Atlantic Monthly, Harper's*, a few others. Many of those magazines are very good and frequently run articles about the shittiness of other businesses, but they rarely pick up the stones covering their own and see what's underneath. And most of the little magazines I publish in would love to be big enough magazines to need subscription agencies.

What I wonder, from the perspective of so many years, is who is actually responsible for this. The magazines? The subscription dealers? The buyers? I always wondered the same thing about Vietnam: who was responsible? The president? Congress? The people who pay taxes?

For me, in those days, a job was a job was a job and I did not question either the morality of the people who were exploiting me or my own exploitation of the women, and in those days they were almost all women, who came to the door when I knocked on it. Nor did I question the morality of the publishers who would have had to have been blind not to know that that whole series of exploitation was going on.

grabbed my hand and pulled me out onto the floor. "Come on, baby, you're 10 years old, closest thing to a man in here except for your daddy. 'Bout time you learned how to do this." She grabbed my right arm and pulled it around her waist and held my left hand in hers. "Just move to the music, baby, feel the rhythm." She started to move, pulling me with her, my feet dragging along behind me. The song was "Jambalaya" and after a slow lead in it sped up. I felt her fling me away into a kind of strange jitterbug. "Just move in an out with the beat for now," she said and pulled me towards her and then pushed away. I couldn't help it. When she pulled me in, I smashed into her stomach and breasts. She pushed me back hard and I fell into a table and knocked it over as I crashed with it down to the dirty floor.

"Maybe next year," she laughed. My father pulled me up and sat me back down in the booth and the two of them finished the dance. I wiped my hands on my jeans. The floor had been dirty and sticky and when I rubbed my eyes, I got whatever it was on my face. I drank the last of my soda and, still blurry-eyed, watched them. As he twirled her around he kept his beer bottle in his hand and drank from it. They moved quickly, in and out, the music seeming to drive them around the floor. I couldn't understand how anyone could move like they were moving. He winked at me as if to say, "This is how it's done."

When the tenth song played, "Running Bear" or "Fraulein" or something like that, we went back out to the car. My father sang a verse of "Honky-tonk Angels," and then dug out of the parking lot almost veering into the ditch on the other side of the highway. My mother lit a cigarette and didn't bother to hold it out the window. "Gotta teach that boy how to dance," she said.

My father just drank and nodded. In spite of the way he loved to dig out of a parking lot, he always drove slowly when he'd had too much and as I looked out the back seat window I could see the trunks of the trees near the road passing by and the darkness of the undergrowth. My father stopped the car in Kountze and bought two more beers. He drank deeply as he drove and sang along with the radio all the way back to Beaumont and home.

Washed In the Blood

When I was twelve years old, I was saved, born again, washed in the blood, taken into the bosom of the Lord after being preached over by Brother Noble Lawrence in a small Southern Baptist Church in Beaumont, Texas. I do not want to make light of this since it was a big event in my life, the biggest up until then.

My family had been attending Memorial Baptist Church each Sunday and sometimes on Wednesday nights for the past four years. I looked forward to Sundays, days when I would receive ratification as one of the rising stars among the children in the congregation. If the days were wet and cold, then the sacrifice was even greater and my pleasure in going to church, in some ways, made even finer.

We would arrive at the small, white, clapboard building at 8 a.m. and my brother, my sister and I would be hustled into Sunday School, different rooms for each age. There we would learn Bible verses, color pictures of scenes from the Bible, sing religious music, mostly songs that have stuck with me, songs like "Jesus loves the little children, / all the children of the world" and "Jesus loves me, this I know / for the Bible tells me so." I enjoyed the singing and was a whiz of a scripture memorizer. By the time I achieved apostasy, I had committed more than a thousand verses to memory. But that was still four years in the future.

When I was twelve, I was a true believer. After Sunday School, we would move with our family into the church proper to sit in hard pews and listen to Brother Lawrence thunder the week's message at us. He was a classic Baptist orator with a big, booming voice and a form of terrible lyricism as he talked to us of the pains of Hell and the sweet rewards of Heaven. It was not possible not to listen to him and even when I did not understand all the words I did understand both the threat and the promise.

That threat and that promise would be repeated at revivals every other month or so—a whole week of going to church in a tent—and, during the summers, at Vacation Bible School and weekend church camps.

But, as with most church services everywhere, the sermon was not the only part of the Sunday service. The first half of the service was a mix of singing and praying and responses that were written in bold face in the day's service order. Brother Lawrence was always in the front of the church and he would call on men, always men, to lead the congregation in prayer. I had always assumed the designated man was informed in advance and prepared the prayer, perhaps spending hours getting it right before standing up and saying it, and I had looked forward to leading the congregation in prayer when I grew up. But that was not how it happened. Praying during the service was, instead, supposed to be extemporaneous, improvisational, perhaps inspired. I have always thought, though, that most of the men did prepare, had some idea of what and with which words they were going to pray, just in case they were called on. Those "unrehearsed" prayers were directly responsible for one of the moments in my life for which I remain most ashamed.

One morning, fresh out of Sunday school, having memorized the next Sunday's twelve verses between class and the regular church service, I walked into Memorial Baptist Church with my mother, father, sister and brother and sat through the music. I always sang loudly, much more than likely out of tune, and read the responses with great feeling and gusto. I was an insufferable little prig, snotty and devout at the same time. I was, in short, a true believer and, paradoxically, proud of it.

Brother Lawrence had never before called on my father to pray, but that morning he did. My father, who was essentially a shy man, a good man who had gone through hard times, shook his head and I heard him whisper, "Call on someone else, not me," but could tell that the preacher did not hear. I was incredibly embarrassed and only years later would be terribly ashamed of myself for my reaction. I went into a deep sulk, disappointed and, disgracefully, ashamed of my father. For a moment, only a brief moment, I considered standing up and praying myself. After all, I, too, was Brother Hall, though the preacher had not yet called me by my surname.

During that period of perceived disgrace, I memorized whole chapters of the New Testament. The Old Testament would not do. I was evidently a very selective Biblical scholar as I seem not to have remembered, *Exodus* 20:12, "Honor your father and your mother, that your days may be long upon the land which the Lord your God has given you." Or even *Deuteronomy* 5: 16, "Honor your father and mother as the Lord your God has commanded you." Those were, of course, in the Old Testament, but the New Testament does not provide much relief: Matthew reminds us in Chapter 15, verse 4 "For God commanded, saying "Honor your father and mother." And Mark chimes in with a slight variation in attribution (*Mark* 7:10) "For Moses said, Honor your father and your mother."

My father never said anything about that day, but I know he felt deeply shamed by the whole thing. By coincidence, or so I assumed at that time, the very next Sunday, when Brother Lawrence ended another lengthy, bombastic sermon and called those who were saved to come to the front of the Church, I felt myself moved by the spirit and left the pew to walk up. The next week, I would wear a shirt and tie, the first time I ever wore a tie, and be led by the preacher into the pool of water behind the glass wall at the very front of the Church and be totally immersed, one of his hands behind my back, the other on my head, as he held and pushed me beneath the water to wash my sins away. Wanting to see God's spirit enter me, I kept my eyes open while I was under water. What I saw was the preacher's arm, bubbles of air around each hair, and the light from the bare bulb that could not be seen by the congregation, but created what I considered a sacred shimmer at the joining of water and air. For whatever reason, the baptism took and I felt more saved than I had ever felt in my life.

Afterwards, still wet, the whole congregation welcomed me into fellowship. I must have been impossibly saintly and incredibly difficult to live with for weeks afterwards. Though I cannot remember much about those weeks, I know I amen-ed people a lot, quoted a lot of scripture, tried to pray, like Franny Glass, incessantly and I know that I did not want to take my wet clothes off when we finally got home and that I rather resented my mother's insistence. But I did not say the Matthew prayer, did not say, "Lord Jesus Christ, have mercy on me, a miserable sinner." I was so puffed up with my own holiness that I knew I was no longer a miserable sinner.

When I was sixteen, I left the Baptist and all other churches. I cannot say exactly why, and it was not abrupt, more of a slow drift away. I only know that I became alienated from my past life, from that community, from that kind of place. But among the reasons, surely, was my realization, even then, that that whole string of events when I had been ashamed of my father and should have been ashamed of myself, began to prey on me and I no longer truly believed much of anything that anyone, especially preachers, had to say to me.

I have thought about those events often since my father died forty-one years ago. And during many of those years I grew in cynicism. My father had, himself, been born again the year before I walked down the center aisle of the church and it had been a wonderful transformation for the whole family. He gave up drinking, stayed home more, became, in short, a man who was dedicated to his family and to his God. We no longer feared, when he came home from the sea, that he would take off his belt and punish us for all the transgressions we had committed while he was away. I know now that he could not have enjoyed those moments, the feeling that his was the belt of retribution, the terrible swift sword, in our family, but at that time, my brother and I rarely looked forward to his return from whatever ship he had been on. That change, in him and in me, is something I will always thank the Baptist church and Brother Lawrence for.

Earlier in that same year when he was finally called upon to pray in church, he had pledged a thousand dollars to the church building fund—dollars that the family could not afford. There was Christmas that year, but no presents. A tree with nothing under it. I know that sounds petty, especially for a boy who would soon be a devout, born again Baptist, well on his way to becoming a Royal Ambassador and, perhaps, a Baptist preacher or, even better in my thoughts at that time, a foreign missionary off to China or Africa to win souls for Jesus, but Christmas that year went to the church fund. I cannot help but suspect that Brother Lawrence's finally calling upon my father to pray was a direct result of that donation and that the preacher thought it was a just reward. The fact that it was more of a punishment would not have occurred to him.

A few years after leaving the church, I spent a 365-day tour in Vietnam and, while I was not in combat, I did hug the ground on a few occasions listening to the thump-thump-thump of mortars and of rockets landing in our compound. At those times, as frightened as any of the other men huddled on the ground, I did not erupt into prayer or rediscover God in a bunker. Rather than finding God in their version of foxholes, many of the men I met there and have met since who did serve, in and out of combat, found themselves without faith in much of anything after their tours.

Still, twenty-three years later I did go to church again and to a church that would have been anathema to Brother Lawrence—the Catholic Church. When I stopped going to Memorial Baptist, I had tried others for a few months: a Methodist church, Presbyterian, Episcopal. But none of them had much appeal. So, for more than two decades, I did not enter a church at all.

I did not decide at any point that there was no God; I simply did not care and certainly no longer believed in the Baptist hell nor in the pictures of heaven that Brother Lawrence had so adroitly painted. The "NP," no preference, on my dog tags said it all.

When I finally did return to church, in 1978, it was because my son had been born and my wife attended the Catholic Church regularly. Later, after a long association with the men and women who make up the Society of Mary, the religious order that sponsors and continues to be important in the university where I work, I became a real believer. Perhaps I was just one small part of a sociological trend documented on the cover of *Time* magazine some years ago: the return of the "baby boom" generation to the church. I returned for the old, old reason: family unity. Perhaps there was a renewed "calling" with the birth of my son or, maybe, deep down inside, I simply wanted my son to have something to rebel against, just as I had had. That I have more than received.

Still, though, when I find myself needing contact with the spiritual I rarely find it inside church walls. Instead, I go back to Southeast Texas, where I was born and attended church, to spend time in the Big Thicket National Preserve or I drive south to Matagorda Island. Those places are clean and fresh, even after decades of clear cutting in the thicket and the World War II Army Air Corp's bombing of the island. The sound of the wind blowing through the sea oats on the island, the waves rushing onto shore, or the strange cry of a pileated woodpecker back in the thicket speak truths that I have not yet fully learned to translate. I can lose myself in those places, those sounds, without ever being truly lost and in those places I find myself.

Coming To Terms

I have always found it difficult to talk about that moment, but as a teenager I lost something very important to me. No, not one of my parents, not my brother or sister, something, though, that I was a part of. And something I find difficult to talk about. It all happened forty years ago and I still have problems when I drive through that stretch of highway and woods between Beaumont and Silsbee. Let me tell you about it this way. When I was growing up I was both fortunate enough and unfortunate enough to live near the Big Thicket of Southeast Texas where my ancestors, most named Hooks, had lived since the 1840s...

Vernon Dugard had returned from Mississippi and Alabama. He had grown up, grown quickly after a few months riding on Freedom Buses through Mississippi and Alabama. This was a few years after the Brown v. Board of Education decision was rendered by the U.S. Supreme Court. Three of his friends had been brutally murdered, but this is not about them. Vernon was teaching at Silsbee High School, a school that many of his relatives and ancestors had attended: his parents and his parents' parents, though their schoolhouse had been smaller, much smaller. I would teach at Silsbee High School only a few years later.

I had not met my cousin-by-marriage Vernon until that fall. I had spent much of that summer hiking into the Thicket. I had aimed at but not shot three whitetail deer, had caught fish to eat and found artesian springs to drink from, had learned to live on my own in the woods for two solid weeks. I had, at seventeen years old, lived apart from the world and in a part of the world that would permit me to forget or ignore all of the problems Vernon had been fighting.

Vernon brought me up to date. The two of us spent weeks talking about his days in Mississippi, hot, threatening, and then the disappearance of his friends. "We thought they'd been burned up in the car," Vernon had said. "But there were no bodies there." I listened to my cousin. When he walked back to his tent close to the creek, I thought about what he had said. I thought about a society that would murder young men and women Vernon's age because they were working for other people's rights to vote and be treated like everyone else.

You see, we took a lot for granted in Beaumont, Texas, even while not consciously thinking about what was happening in our society. We went into restaurants and were served by people who could not eat at the same tables they served our food on. We went to movies and sat on the main floor while they sat in the balconies. We saw ourselves on television and movie screens; they saw us, too. They went to, were bused to, separate and unequal schools. We were the city councilmen, mayors, policemen; they did not often get to cast their vote. Vernon and I talked about a lot of things that summer when I was graduating from high school and getting ready to go to college.

I did my undergraduate work at Lamar State College of Technology, later renamed Lamar University. Lamar was an early experiment in integration of state universities in Texas and it worked reasonably well. Oh, many of the white students bitched a lot and whites and blacks re-segregated themselves at various tables in the cafeteria, but, basically, things went fairly well: no major demonstrations, no riots. Some of the home-grown faculty members were worse problems than any of the students. D. L. Hybarger, who had been principal of my segregated high school taught on the education faculty and I dropped his "methods" course because of his treatment of a young black woman in the class. She was stunningly beautiful and, on the first day of class, Hybarger asked her why she hadn't been caught already by some "strong young black buck." My consciousness had not yet been raised but I was so offended by his question that I stood up immediately and went to the registrar's office to drop the course and add a different one.

I was a speech and drama major and there were a few black students in the field. None on the stage as performers until my second year in the school. We always had cast parties at the same place: The Golden Arrow, owned and managed by Red Shelton, a rather florid and demonstrative man who always welcomed us with open arms. The Arrow had some of the best chicken fried steak in the State of Texas and I had a running tab there. That first night we arrived with one of the black women from a play, it was, ironically enough, *The Diary of Anne Frank*, Red told us we were no longer welcome unless she left.

At moments like that I always thought about Vernon and the experiences he had gone through in Mississippi during the freedom rides. You see, I was not terribly enlightened. I just had not thought very much about the whole black/white issue in my corner of the South. In retrospect, I would say that I was incredibly dense, perhaps even willfully not looking at what was there, at what was so easy to see if anyone simply looked. Vernon was slowly opening my eyes, encouraging me to focus them.

In my last year as an undergraduate, I participated in a sit-in at Morgan & Lindsay's in Beaumont, Texas. That was early in 1963. The public schools were not yet integrated, black people could not sit at the fountain in Morgan & Lindsay's and get a soda, only whites sat at the front of the bus, there were still "White" and "Colored" water fountains at the Greyhound Bus Station. Jesus Christ! That was a great day in my life. We sat very peacefully at the fountain until the police came and ordered us out of the store. That doesn't sound like much. We were not beaten, not tear gassed, not locked up in the city jail, just taken by the arms and led out of the store to accompanying newspaper photographs and stories. My picture isn't there and I'm not mentioned in the story. I was pretty much on the periphery of the whole "movement," but it all remains so important, something that we should not, cannot fail to remember.

I guess I'm writing all this because Vernon died 35 years ago and I am thinking about him today. He was still teaching at that high school up in the thicket, still doing good work, still an advocate for whatever he believed in. He had stopped to change a flat on the shoulder of Highway 169, the road that leads from Beaumont out to Jasper, the town where James Byrd, Jr., would be murdered so many years later, when a car swerved off the road and killed him. Hit and run. The police never found the driver or the car. No, it wasn't deliberate murder. I'm pretty sure of that. Just one of those horrible incidents that remind us of how fragile we can be, of how good people can just vanish from our lives in an eye blink. This, too, is important. That we stop in our lives from time to time just to sit back and remember good people, people who, in quiet ways, made a difference.

Before Going To Vietnam

New York, 1964. I am working at the World's Fair in Flushing Meadows and, though I am not terribly fond of the job, I love New York. Slathering mustard and relish on hot dogs, making change, listening to complaints about the expense, hearing hundreds of dialects and languages, I am not impressed with the fair. My feet hurt. My eyes hurt. My sense of smell is incredibly dulled. I go to see the Pieta: alabaster woman, son lying across her lap-so white, so pale. And yet protected by bulletproof glass, my feet on a moving sidewalk that draws me quickly through the room. Not New York, Disneyland, long before Disney cleaned up Times Square.

I live at the Dixie Hotel, a few blocks off Times Square and I have a girlfriend, Sharon, I met at the Fair. Years later, I wrote a poem for Sharon, an aubade, a morning poem:

There should be flowers, sweet fragrances
the buzzing of bees. When I wake, your bottom
hot against my groin, the sun has got to rise,
golden beautiful in the east, to paint your body.

But we are in the Dixie Hotel, a block or two
off Times Square and the windows are streaked
with grime from back before the war, no,
not that war, I mean the second of the two.

No air conditioning and the ceiling fan doesn't
work any more if it ever did back when the Dixie
was fairly swank if such times ever were. We've
left the window open, can hear the sounds

not of sweet birds and of crickets rubbing their legs
together, but of cabs and buses, the crashing
of garbage trucks. Still, your body touches mine, and even
with this dawn, this heat, the air in the room barely

moving, we can sing the morning in, ignore dark soot,
let our fingers draw lines of damp sweat on naked canvas.

Ah, love, outside noise and hot streets call,
but let's remain a while, here, in this still morning.

I take long walks any time of the night and day. No one ever mugs me. On the day I arrived, I was insulted, but the old woman was crazy. She heard my voice, assumed I was from Texas and accused me of killing John F. Kennedy. Crazy, I suppose. But I did kill Kennedy, as much as anyone did, anyone in our society of celebrity. He is avenged a few years later when I am sent to Vietnam.

We are all crazy, beyond the grasp of reality. Have you imagined New York is real? Any more than the London Eliot called "Unreal City?" I find New York as I have so often found New Orleans: a dreamworld where I lose myself and become something other.

One day, Sharon and I walk a couple of blocks to the theater district to where Richard Burton is performing *Hamlet*. The building is, for some reason, unlocked. We walk in and see the dark interior. I flip on a light and climb up on the stage; Sharon sits on the front row. "Oh that this too too solid flesh would melt thaw or dissolve itself into a dew," I whisper to her and to a thousand empty seats. I am young, in love again and enamored of theater, and all the seats are full.

I am Hamlet and am in love with everything, even as Hamlet loved everything. He did, you know, he loved everything and truth most of all. "I have been so great a lover," Rupert Brooke says to open one of his poems, and so I have. Later, he would write "If I should die, think only this of me / That there is some corner of some foreign land / That is forever England." I have never been that much of a romantic about war. Perhaps it was just the war that I happened to have. But I have loved the dirty streets of Times Square, a filthy hotel room, the grime of Far Rockaway, a young woman who came onto me one late night in New York and whom I could not afford and would not have afforded could I have.

I see the last acts of a dozen plays. I cannot afford to see the whole play—much too expensive for a young man subsisting in New York on minimum wage. But I find the money to see Burton perform *Hamlet* a few weeks later and continue, so many years later, to think it was worth it. Late at night, long after I have seen Elizabeth Taylor pick Burton up in a limousine, I open my window in the Dixie Hotel and sit on the fire escape. I whisper the "to be or not to be" speech out across the back alley. No air conditioning, no rest room (I go to a common bathroom at the end of the corridor when I need to go). The room is a pale green, some of the paint peeling from the walls. It has a burner and a small fridge. Many of the rooms, I am certain, rent by the hour. I rent mine by the week and manage to make ends meet.

One Sunday I go to a matinee of *Never on Sunday* with Melina Mercouri (I do not mean to imply that Mercouri was my date, she was the star) and I fall in love with her. She is much older than me, but I had also fallen in love with Simone Signouret when I saw her in *Room at the Top*. I am busy falling in love; it is what I do best when I am in my twenties. I fall in love with my cheap hotel room, with small pizza-by-the-slice places, with winos in the crowd, with the pieta (only a passing flirtation), with street musicians, with Central Park, with everything in the city. But Melina Mercouri is both love and lust. I notice nothing around me in the theatre except her and then the man in the seat next to mine gropes me and throws his coat over my lap. I push his hand off and throw his coat back on his own lap, turn to him and say, "No, thank you." He is about sixty-five, I think, and is embarrassed. I am more interested in Melina Mercouri. After her four curtain calls, I leave the theater.

I am not certain I can tell you what my summer in New York meant to me—that summer of the World's Fair, that last summer before I was drafted and sent to Vietnam. That summer in the city, that summer going to the theater, to a few cattle calls, before going back to the southeast corner of Texas to teach high school and then go off to war, that summer living in what I would call poverty had I taken the days in another way of taking something seriously, that summer that comes back to me when I chart where I have been and how I have gotten where I eventually arrived and where I might have arrived had I remained there as something other than a romantic, romanticizing tourist. You see, I loved the Manhattan of 1964. It was dirty, profane, not yet cleaned up by Disney and Associates. I loved the idea of me there in those years before I ever thought of writing and when theatre and love were everything.

It has been too many years for me to remember precisely what New York meant to me when I was a very young twenty-two years old. That is so long ago that I now remember only bright images. But I can remember that young man who walked out of the Dixie

Hotel and wandered over to Radio City where he was offered a job as an NBC Junior Executive (that meant "usher" in those days) and preferred just walking through the streets looking at things, staring up at buildings taller than the pine trees in Southeast Texas, and losing himself in crowded streets and falling soot.

Late that summer, I left New York, hitched a ride to Philadelphia where my uncle had taken up residence with his upper class Philly wife thirty years earlier. Tall at 6' 4" and a certified WWII hero, Purple Heart awardee and member of the renowned "greatest generation," he went to the Wharton School at Penn on the GI Bill and, ultimately, became a steadfast Republican and ally of Governor Scranton. I am not sure Scranton knew who my uncle was, but my uncle dropped his name frequently. I am, I am afraid, being uncharitable to my uncle and he was always kind to me. I don't mind, though, and he's no longer with us. Besides, I drop George McGovern's name probably as often as he dropped Scranton's.

He really wanted me to find a job and settle down in the Philadelphia area. So, it seemed counter-productive to me for him to keep snarling and bitching about how awful Philadelphians were. I mean I could never figure out why he wanted to stay in a place he seemed not to like, much less why he thought what he was saying would influence me to move there. But this isn't about my uncle or even about Philadelphia. It's about young lust and, even, towards the end, about young love.

To that end and to entice me to stay, he set me up with a few girls, daughters of his friends for the most part. One, I remember, had been his kids' baby sitter. All were white, protestant and a year or two younger than me. Each one, except the sitter, had a nice car and belonged to a good club. In that year, 1964, the summer before I would be drafted, the beginnings of the sexual revolution, predating the summer of love by a few years, had already started to emerge. The Beatles had not yet, but were about to, exploded into our consciousness and "All ya need is love" might not have been recorded yet but was an ever-present nagging sound in my mind. And love, love, love was all around.

With my uncle shouting about the undesirables in his neighborhood, I closed my ears and went out with a half dozen young women and groped and snuggled and made love along the river, in their parents' houses when their parents were out for the evening, and almost, once, while the baby sitter was driving across the Walt Whitman Bridge into New Jersey. I am not, really, ashamed of any of that. It was merely the zeitgeist. None of it took for more than a week or two and, after a couple of months, I planned to hitch back to Texas.

Then, with two weeks to go, I went with my uncle and his family for a two-week stay at their beach house on the Jersey coast. I loved the house, even got along with my aunt's mother when we visited and putt-putted around with my cousin in his small boat. And there were more girls and, as always, they were enticing, but only one stays with me. I walked along the beach with Connie whose last name I cannot remember even though I do remember that the water seemed strangely cold for August and not at all like the waters of the Gulf of Mexico. I can remember her touch, the warmth of her skin, even a small dimple, but not her name. Somehow, that seems sad to me. I suspect she doesn't remember my name either but does remember some boy from Texas she spent time with one summer in Avalon.

I did not have to hitch a ride back to Texas. My uncle was generous and bought an airline ticket for me, the first time I had ever flown. And I'm pretty sure the plane was a DC-3. In Vietnam a few years later, we called them C-47s. I suspect my uncle was pleased to get rid of me and had changed his mind about the possibilities of finding me a good job in Philly.

Back in Beaumont, I met Jenny. Jenny was unlike any other woman I had met up until that time. She was ahead of her time and definitely ahead of mine, too. A few decades later, I wrote a poem for her. It's never been published, probably because it's pretty bad, and I don't have it here with me for some strange reason, but here's a rough approximation:

My Jenny wears an eagle / tattoed on her ass…

Well, that's how it begins and it has a weird kind of celebratory encantation for an ending. This is something like it: "Jenny is my darling / Jenny is my dear / Jenny turns the boy's on / whenever she gets near. // Jenny's got an eagle / but she bares it just for me / and …." Well, it goes on and on. I never said it was a good poem, but it was a lot better than that particular rip-off of the poem. You see, the mid to late sixties were my *annas mirabilis* or however you spell the damned words. And I guess I never got over them. Most of the girls I knew then, and we did not call them women in the mid-sixties, I have written at least one poem for and I do not want anyone to think I was some kind of Don Juan or Wilt Chamberlain and certainly not a Kobe Bryant. I could barely make a decent-sized chapbook of them! There weren't really all that many—I just remember each one fairly well.

"An aged man is but a paltry thing," William Butler Yeats said in "Sailing to Byzantium"—but the memories are worth revisiting from time to time.

Walking

> *O body swayed to music, O brightening glance,*
> *How can we know the dancer from the dance?*
> —William Butler Yeats

I get on the treadmill and walk when it is cold or rainy and I walk for pleasure on other days–through the neighborhood, in state parks, on campus, on golf courses. And I am physically more fit than I have been in years, in spite of heart surgery, and well-tanned from the South Texas sun. I am reminded of "Among School Children" by William Butler Yeats though I am not as old as Yeats was when he wrote that amazing poem. Amazing because of the sheer glory of the language and because of the truth it contains. I think, too, of a poem I wrote when I was a freshman in college and its rhymed couplet ending: "I was alive, but running it away / in a sea of blinding, dying day." That very young and romantic couplet, which owes so much to Dylan Thomas, is filled with the angst of youth. In the middle and later years, though, the angst remains even if we rarely speak of it and we more often walk than run.

When I was a small boy and living summers at Wakulla Beach, not too far from Tallahassee, Florida, I often ran or walked four or five hundred yards from my grandmother's house down to the bay. The place was inhabited by dozens of varieties of snakes, rumors of panthers, wild hogs gone feral in that wilderness area that would, only a few years later, become the St. Mark's National Wildlife Preserve. It embraced alligators in small ponds and in the bay, and in the air hawks, vultures, so many different kinds of wild things.

I remember leaping over a small barbed-wire fence that ran half way down to the beach because a feral hog with tusks had raced after me. I suspect he could have crossed the fence and was probably just warning me away from young pigs. I stood on one side of the fence and watched him on the other. He was big and actually dug at the sand road with one of his feet, almost like the movie scenes of bulls in the ring. I walked on down to the beach, but stayed on the other side of the fence from the road.

Each day, I would walk two miles up the road toward U.S. Highway 98 to get the mail. The Post Office refused to take it as far down that little road as my family lived. That was always a fairly spooky trip, but still lovely. I'd walk under old oaks trailing Spanish moss or by cabbage palms with dried fronds circling their bases. The water in the ditches on either side of the road was clear but streaked with dark brown from the tannin leaching from pine trees.

There is something about a deep wilderness area, even one with a sandy road running through it, that whispers of both the beginnings and endings of things. In that area my grandfather and his father had grown up and died and my father had been born and gone to school. I went back almost every year to visit and to walk until I was in my twenties and my grandmother died.

I have always been a fairly solitary person though I enjoy the company of good friends. But when I go into the wilderness or into the Texas Hill Country for a long walk, I prefer solitude, just as, so many years ago, I preferred to take that long walk to the mailboxes alone. There was always something new to see: wild turkeys on one side of the road, a small fox racing across the road in front of me, a diamondback rattlesnake coiled beneath a palmetto. And myself, if we can truly see ourselves, a small boy of nine or ten, alone on a sandy road in the middle of a fifty-square mile wilderness area, barefoot, dusty blond hair, feeling almost a part of the rest of the life that belonged in that area.

When I was seven, on one of my walks down to the beach, I spotted an old tin can that someone had dropped alongside the road. It made me angry to see it and I kicked it, planning to pick it up on the way back to throw it away. But I caught it wrong on my foot and cut a deep gash into my big toe. I walked back to my grandmother's house, dropping blood onto the road, and, I am sure, crying. My father gave me the choice of going to the doctor or letting him take care of the cut. I did not want to go to the doctor. I almost changed my mind, too late, when my father opened the wound and poured iodine from a dark brown bottle over it. He wrapped it tight in gauze and strips of tape and, later, I could only feel it throbbing.

Years later, the scar still visible on my toe, mortars fell on my hooch outside of Pleiku and a ricocheting fragment hit my other toe. For a while I had matching scars though the physical Vietnam scar faded more quickly. Both of those scars still throb, in a way, from time to time.

These days, when I have the time, I drive miles to find a place I want to walk. I have walked through the Lost Maples along the Medina River, a small river in Texas only a few yards wide, and on an old ranch in the Hill Country that has become Hill Country State Park or along the Pedernales River and down the beach on Mustang Island and Matagorda Island.

It may seem odd to drive so many miles just to get out of the car and walk. But I have seen an eagle fly in the Hill Country and dolphins near the islands and leaves turn red on maple trees. And I have been alone with all this, free to be a part of it without having to tell anyone else what I am thinking. That's worth the long drives.

Walking Out On Things

I did not walk out on *Forrest Gump* though I absolutely resented his lengthy speech at the end of the film. After sitting through hours of crap to enjoy minutes of the movie, the audience got to experience a restating of the whole damned thing in a monologue almost guaranteed to bring tears to the eyes of anyone who wasn't being sick at the time. I found that speech incredibly insulting. Almost, but not quite, as insulting as the 100+ page section of Ayn Rand's *Atlas Shrugged* entitled "This Is John Galt Speaking." Remember that? You have just read more than a thousand pages of capitalistic ideological posturing, the sex scenes closely resembling "getting off" on corporate mergers—you know what the book is about, yes, you do, you understand it deep down in the bowels where all true understanding occurs. BUT, Rand considers you stupid. She writes a 100-page essay to explain what the comic book you have just read actually means. Gump does that, too, and it is insulting.

I have walked out on things before. In 1963 or 1964 (I forget which) I walked out on *Your Cheating Heart* (I think that was the name of the BioFlick of Hank Williams's life). But not just because the movie was awful and sentimental. You see, I had this "date," a girl I had been seeing for a few months and in those days we called young women "girls"—this is not meant to be a political statement. Those of you who have been fortunate enough to see *Your Cheating Heart* (and I did love the music) will remember that Hank is scheduled to perform in Nashville one night, a terrible night in the history of country-western music. But he is drunk and he is driving. His car goes off the road and Hank goes to that grand old opry in the sky. We shift back to the stage where an aging, crusty announcer silences the audience and then, with everyone hushed, informs them that Hank has been killed. One by one, members of the audience rise to their feet. No, they do more than rise to their feet. They begin to sing. They begin to sing an old Hank Williams song. They are crying, yes, crying, and they are singing, oh, surely not "Your Cheating Heart," that seems so inappropriate, and not "Kalijah" or "Jambalaya," something appropriate.

Okay, probably it was "Your Cheating Heart." But that's not really the point is it? The point is, and I suspect I should be deeply ashamed of this, but I am not, the point is that "my date," the girl I was with, a girl I had been to bed with and thought I had cared about, and this I am somewhat ashamed of, my date began to BOO-HOO right there in the chair next to me. And, lordy, lordy, lordy, I was embarrassed. I considered laughing out loud, but was afraid the singing congregation would turn on me. So, instead, I leaned over and whispered, "I'm outta here" or something like that. I walked out on the movie, the girl, the popcorn, everything. That was, I suppose, in some way, a political statement or, maybe, just a cultural statement.

But I did not walk out on *Forrest Gump*. I walked out on a priest once and on masses a variety of times. The priest was doing communion and when Stephen held his hands the wrong way, the priest made an issue of it, saying something like, "You are old enough to know how to do this." He grabbed Stephen's hands and pulled them up. I grabbed the priest's hands and said, "I'd rather not be in communion with you, thanks," and walked out with Stephen. I explained to Stephen that priests are, generally, about like anyone else and that you find a certain number of assholes in any population group.

But, generally, my walking out is pretty passive. I walk out on a book I don't like, by closing it, then selling it to Half-Price Books. I walk out on a bad discussion list on the internet by unsubscribing. I walked out on the whole world of television a few years ago by not turning my set on. No one notices; no one cares.

I did not walk out on *Forrest Gump*. I thought the movie was pretty average, not great, but guaranteed to inspire some response: either approval or strong negation. I am not surprised that it did just that. It is a movie almost impossible to shrug off. I would not watch the film again and I am not fond of its book author, Winston Groom. Groom wrote a Vietnam War novel, *Better Times Than These* (I think that's the title) that I thought played the same kind of sentimental tricks.

I don't walk out on a lot of things. Twelve years ago, when we got a new president at the university where I work and he decided the budget needed to be cut, he called each of us who is a "budget director" before his budget team to "discuss" the budget. The upshot of it was that no one was going to discuss the budget. A decision had been made. The president said, "We need to cut the library budget by 10%." I said, "Well, we do need to talk about what can be done." The financial VP said, "No, we're cutting the budget by 10%." I said, "Then we're not discussing anything, right? You've already decided without knowing what the university actually needs in terms of library services." The president said, "No, we want to talk about it." I said, "But the 10% cut is going to happen anyway?" He said, "Yes." At that point, I stood up and said, "We have nothing to discuss. This is just a stage setting." I walked out and slammed the door. I also had another job lined up for the next month as director of the main branch of the public library, but that's another boring story. Nothing happened to me. That year, all five of our deans were fired (deservedly, I thought) and every director except me was fired. Two years later, that president was fired by the Board of Trustees. I don't think there's a real moral to this tale, some lesson to be learned. Just another "walking out" story. Now, it sounds like it has a moral. You know: always speak your mind and stand up for what you believe in, son, things'll work out." But that's not what it was really about. It was about my being pissed off. And our president was just perverse enough not to fire me.

I didn't walk out on Vietnam, though I turned against it. I didn't walk out on graduate school or teaching. When I walk out on something, it's usually a spur of the moment thing. Walking out on the girl and the movie and the popcorn and stuff was spontaneous. Walking out on the president and the budget team was like shooting the finger at them. Momentary things. No moral there. I guess *Forrest Gump* just didn't offend me enough.

Teaching High School English

A few months after the assassination of John F. Kennedy, I graduated from Lamar State College of Technology (since renamed, in a glut of remorse over that lesser identity, Lamar University) and, at 20 years old, began to teach at a small high school in the Big Thicket of Southeast Texas. Silsbee High School was country: the largest club was the Future Farmers of America and that club also had the biggest and wildest parties along with most of the high school football players. Some of the Ag. Students in Silsbee were only a year younger than I was and most of them were much larger and stronger. The largest of those students was a young man named James Collins, fullback (19-years old), for the Silsbee Tigers. His great great great grandfather and mine had both hidden out in the Big Thicket a hundred years earlier to avoid being drafted into the Confederate Army (not because they were pro-Union, but because they thought the War of the Rebellion was a rich planters' war that had little to do with their lives).

I began teaching speech and English in Silsbee because of the unfortunate experiences of my predecessor in the job. She had been unable to "control" the class and, on several occasions, had fainted dead away after her screaming at the students had had no effect on them. She resigned in frustration and for her health just before Christmas, 1963, and returned to Arkansas.

When I walked into the high school in early January, 1964, I thought I had entered a monkey house. No one was seated in a chair, no one was particularly attentive, two of the students were sitting on a window ledge letting their legs dangle down, no one seemed to think they had any purpose except to mark time. That first class was a 'remedial' English class and the accustomed work was to fill out worksheets that focused on such things as comma faults, run-on sentences, faulty parallelism and other problems upon which the fate of the English-speaking world quite obviously depended. I was also expected to give a spelling test once a week.

Young and still somewhat idealistic, I was having none of that. When I want to I can project what my students in Silsbee called a BOOMing voice and that first day I BOOMed at them until they had returned to their seats and began to look at me as if I were some

Martian landed and ready to bear arms against them. Of the 30 students in that remedial class, my predecessor had flunked 27, all boys, all members of FFA. I could not help thinking that much of the problem had been hers for not taking firmer control of the class.

The first thing I did was announce that any student who did well in that spring semester, who actually began to work at something close to grade level, would receive a passing grade for the full year. I saw little point in beginning something that ensured that more than half the class would fail. The second thing I did was have them tear up their workbooks. I could think of nothing more boring and more guaranteed to keep students from learning than fifty minutes each day spent filling in blanks on worksheets.

Instead of having them spend their time on something that obviously was not working, I asked them to write about their families, their parents, their grandparents; about how they had come to be living in Silsbee and the thicket. We did workshop groups before I had even heard the term and they began to enjoy the work. I do not, in any way, want to suggest that they became "good" writers or that I was some kind of super-teacher, only that they did begin to work hard and they did improve.

I taught in the Silsbee Independent School District for a year and a half and most of that work was with remedial classes. I did, however, have one class each year in drama and was responsible for directing two student plays (full-length) and one one-act play for district and state competition each year. One of my "stars" that first half year was James Collins from my first period remedial English (we had not yet learned to call it developmental) class. He was a good-looking young man, great body (all that football practice), super tan, about 6' 3" tall. I cast him as "the young man" in Edward Albee's "The Sandbox" for the one-act play competition and while he had little to do except look good on stage while doing various types of calisthenics, he did that beautifully.

My problem with James was that he was a very young 19 and wanted to giggle while he was on stage for the preview before the whole student body. He also developed a full-body blush from wearing nothing but a skimpy, brief, swimsuit in front of his peers. For most of the young women in the school, James was *the* student "body." Other cast members were Gail Overland as "granny," Diane Stevens as "mommy," and Mike Stewart as "daddy."

Diane was a very blonde, very pretty, young woman who had recently transferred into the school from Portland, Oregon. I fell a little bit in love with her that year when I took her and the rest of the class to the Alley Theater in Houston to see Paul Zindel's The Effect of Gamma Rays on Man-in-the-Moon Marigolds. She was the last person I dropped off when we got back to Silsbee and when she leaned over to kiss me goodnight, my career, such as it was, flashed in front of me and in spite of desire and long before any spasm could occur, I got out of the car and walked around to open her door.

The University Interscholastic League One-Act Play contest was extremely cut throat. Speech teachers from all over the district harangued each other about the rules and I suspect some even tried to bribe the judges. Perhaps one of the reasons I got out of high school teaching was that I did not like that aspect of the whole thing. After all, play directors were not like football coaches (our jobs did not depend on a won/lost record, nor did our salaries go up because of the time we spent on the plays. I continue to think that's unjust, but that's how it was.)

Gail, Diane, Mike and James were excellent in the play. All but James made the District All-Star Cast (Best Actor in a Supporting Role, Mike; best Actress, Diane; best Actress in a Supporting Role, Gail). In spite of that, the play came in second to a 25-minute segment from Richard III. When I asked the judges how our play could have three of the four all-star cast members and not win, the lead judge said the play was simply too short. *C'est la vie de la theatre*!

I quit teaching high school at the end of the spring semester in 1965 to go to graduate school at the University of Texas in Austin. The Superintendent of the SISD wrote the Selective Service Board, within a week of my resignation, that I was no longer a teacher and was, therefore, eligible for the draft. But I did not receive my GREETING until after I had rented an apartment in Austin and purchased textbooks for the fall semester.

Country Music, Language and Me

I've been thinking about country music and about the kind of language I grew up with. I don't know exactly why I've been thinking of country music, I don't listen to that much anymore, but there it is. The language I grew up not with but in would probably be called a combination of black semi-rural English and poor white trash. Somehow the two things go together in my mind. Most of the Texas country music I heard growing up was sung in the language my relatives spoke back in the Big Thicket and it seemed natural to us. Like a number of my economically disadvantaged friends, I trained it out of my voice as I got older and decided to make Englishing a career. It's not just poor blacks that are limited by their dialect, poor white folks also need to speak standard English to catch a break.

When I grew up, we always had radio station KTRM going in our house. KTRM looms big in my past. A friend of mine in high school, Allen Rayne, was a disk jockey there and the station was run by J. P. Richards. As a country musician "Jape" was best known probably for singing "From a Beggar to a King." But he was much better known under his *nom de rockstar*: the Big Bopper and for singing "Chantilly Lace." According to Allen, Richards was a good man, kind and considerate and was much more the singer of "Beggar to a King" than he ever was of "Chantilly Lace."

KTRM's become a kind of right wing talk radio station in the intervening years, but in those days it always had country and western music of a kind that Waylon Jennings and others would call Texas swing some years later. You'll remember Waylon's song about the honky tonks in Texas. That lyric describes the Southeast Texas country I grew up in. My whole family would drive to small bars up in the country every weekend, "just goin' for a little ride," and listen to Texas swing and other country music, even Nashville stuff. Tex Ritter's brother was my dentist and my father loved Tex's music and Hank Snow's and Hank Williams's...that whole lost band of Texes and Hanks that sang and headed down the highways with cheatin' hearts and songs that had a sob somewhere at their centers.

But the music was in the language. It was in the spoken sounds of the black and white people of Southeast and East Texas, the songs of Mance Lipscomb, of Robert Lee Hooker, of Janis Joplin and Johnny Winter, of "Jape" Richards and the Big Bopper. The music grew from the language spoken in the churches, homes, streets of Beaumont, Texas; Lake Charles, Louisiana; Woodville, Kountze, Spurger, Silsbee. We grew up speaking it and singing it and when the speech stopped we could not always tell when the music actually started.

When I was sixteen and seventeen, my friends and I would drive east past Orange, Texas, and just across the Sabine River to western Louisiana where the age limit was eighteen but no one ever bothered to check Ids. We could go to Lou Ann's or the Big Oaks and listen to Fats Domino and Jimmy Clanton (remember "Little Boy in Love"?) and Chuck Berry and other singers who'd reach deep down inside for their music and release it directly into our souls.

We'd get just drunk enough that we'd dance with the older Louisiana women who hung around the bars and, on the long drive home through a blur of deep green trees and streaks of bright white head lights, brag about how close we'd held them during the long, sad ballads. And laugh when they sang songs like "Long, Tall Texan" or "Hot Nuts, Red Hot Nuts." Those were always popular songs just across the river along with almost anything by Bob Wills and the Texas Playboys.

Those days passed a long time ago, but they're the same days that forever marked the music of Janis Joplin and Johnny and Edgar Winter and an old friend of mine named Steve Young. Steve used to play in those bars at night and, during the day, study music formally and sing in the opera.

"I aint goin' there nohow," we'd say. "No one's gonna keep me from going to no dance Saturday night." "We wasn't doin' nothin' wrong and you don't need to be goin' to tell no one anyhow." My language of growing up and it was not easy to get over it. But it was also the language of our music and there's no way to get over that.

Years later, in graduate school, an English major finally, when Susan and I went out in Austin, perhaps to Armadillo World Headquarters or to Threadgill's, I'd hear that language again in the music of Jerry Jeff Walker or Townes Van Zandt or Willie Nelson and, for a few minutes, I'd be back home again. When Jerry Jeff sang "Mr. Bojangles...Mr. Bojangles...," a song later made even more popular by Sammy Davis, Jr., he took me right back to LuAnn's and those long drives through the thicket and swamps leading to the border of Louisiana.

Waylon sang about those days and for those of us who were there; well, we can't hardly help living them all again. Every time you hear one of the songs, when you drive back up into the woods of Southeast Texas, when you're just almost asleep, those times come back and, Lordy, yes, they were hard, but they were good in so many ways.

Driving To Vietnam

In early September, 1965, one month after I lost my teaching deferment, I bought my first new car...a 1964 and a half reddish-orange Mustang convertible. It would cost more today to buy the same car restored to its pristine condition. That same week, after I began making payments ($87/month), I got my notice to report for an induction physical though I wasn't 'officially' drafted and sworn in until December 29 and was then flown directly to Fort Leonard Wood, Missouri.

For the two months between buying the Mustang and being captured by the Army ('*bat linh*,' the Vietnamese word for 'drafted' means 'captured as a soldier'), I spent almost all of my time driving the car. With no real plans, I picked up a friend, filled a cooler with beer, and drove to Miami Beach, top down, sun shining all the way. We had girl friends from college who were living and working in Coral Gables and spent days and nights with them, but most days the four of us tooled around in the convertible, driving as far south as Key West and north to Georgia..

After we left Florida, we drove back west, spending a week in New Orleans, always drinking and driving, sleeping in the car in the Fontainebleau (Font-le-blue, the natives called it) State Park across the lake from New Orleans and driving back in in the afternoons to drink in the Quarter and watch strip shows. I can still clearly remember a stripper named Linda Brigitte who bought me drinks when she found out I'd been drafted. Linda was the only stripper I met who seemed to enjoy her work; the rest did their bumps and grinds on the tops of bars—bored, tired, sagging. Linda still looked young and, at least, pretended to be enthusiastic about her dancing. The rest of New Orleans remains hazy.

We drove the car north on I-55 to St. Louis and then down unknown highways, non-stop, switching off and on in the driver's seat, until we got to New York and crashed for three days at the YMCA, just off Times Square. Then, back across country to Arizona where we had friends in Flagstaff and down through the desert to Tucson where my sister lived and worked at the Rancho Del Rio on Sabino Canyon Road—a resort reputedly frequented by various clans of mobsters. She wrangled a free room for us for a week—the owner sympathizing with the draftee. Across southern New Mexico to El Paso and back to Beaumont, Texas, for Christmas.

The first working day after Christmas, I dropped the Mustang off at the bank. My new salary ($78 a month) would not make the payments. In those few months, I'd put just under 27,000 miles on the car and hundreds of dollars worth of gasoline on my Mobil card. It took me a year and a half to pay off the credit card and the difference between the buy out on the car and the amount I had already paid. I hitched a ride with Allen Hallmark and Molly Fenton to D.C. for language school after basic training. My only transportation for the next two and a half years was bumming rides from friends.

That's my most memorable car...and, yeh, she was brand new, but worn to a frazzle by the time I gave her back to the bank—only a few months old, but as tired and sagging as most of the strippers in New Orleans and with almost as many miles on her.

Basic Training

I got my draft notice shortly after I quit teaching high school in 1965 and before I got my student deferment for grad school at UT. I could probably have gotten out, but what the hell, I figured it was fate and I was so apolitical I don't recall even having thought of Vietnam at that time. I excuse my own ignorance by thinking that most Americans were also fairly ignorant about that war at that time. I was aware enough, though, that I knew there was fighting going on and that I did not want to be anywhere near it.

So, instead of being drafted for two years, I joined for four and an Army guarantee of language school. I also bought the recruiter's spiel that the Army Security Agency was not allowed to be in Vietnam. Ignorance. In January, 1966, headed for Ft. Leonard Wood and Basic, I met Allen Hallmark, a guy who became one my best friends, on the Ozark (R.I.P.) airplane as it took off from Dallas. The back of the seat broke off as it climbed out of Dallas and I fell backwards landing on him.

The Frozen Chosin of Missouri lived up to its reputation that winter and the colonel in charge of the basic battalion had us bused most places instead of making us take long walks in the snow. He was afraid some of us might get hurt and we were needed in Viet-Nam. I was in the 4th platoon, C-1-3, and our platoon was the most fucked up group of people in the whole company. We were last in everything except written testing and proud of it. A weird mix of college grads and street kids from Kansas City and East St. Louis, we developed a strange kind of bond. A huge dude named Carl Mosley was in my squad. He could have set the brigade push up record, but stood up only one push up away from the record and walked away from it. Didn't want to ruin the platoon's record or some other reason.

Basic for me was really two people: a guy named Niemann and another named Mosley. They were very different people and represented for me the polar extremes of draftees the Army 'captured' as they tried to build for the 1965 escalation in Vietnam. Their story for me is bound up with our platoon sergeant, an immigrant named

Stoss. Sergeant Stoss was an odd Basic Training DI. He had immigrated to the States from somewhere in Central Europe and spoke five or six languages. Of those, he was least fluent in English. He was tough, could be nasty, but wasn't willing to put up with a lot of bullshit. Niemann got him fired.

Niemann was a TR0—Training Required Over. A typical 'Sad Sack,' he could do nothing right. The saddest thing about him, though, was that he tried hard to do things like the other men, but just could not. He was about 5' 8" tall and only a little overweight, but on cold mornings, when the temperature fell down into single digits and we had fallen in in front of the barracks, he would always be missing something—his pack, his entrenching tool, his rifle, always something. He'd stand in formation, his nose draining and his shirt not tucked in right, the tail blousing out. As a result we would all have to run back up three flights of stairs and start over, over and over.

The Senior Drill Instructor, a First Sergeant named Matos, had it in for Niemann, wanted to bust him out of the Army with a dishonorable discharge, was continually on his back and on the back of Sergeant Stoss about him. Matos spoke with the company commander and talked him into ordering Stoss to write Niemann up, to say he was deliberately malingering to get out of the Army.

One evening, Stoss called Allen Hallmark and me into his room. He didn't say much, just "I need some help. Matos wants to screw Niemann and I don't write good enough to stop it." I asked what I could do to help and he said, "I tell you what to write. Your college boys, you put it in good English and I send it to Colonel."

I don't remember the letter well enough to quote it. But Stoss told us to write that Niemann wasn't malingering, that he just wasn't mentally or physically able to keep up with the Company, that he tried hard, but was simply incompetent, that he did not deserve any discharge other than medical or general or, maybe, administrative at the very worst. When we finished, the letter was two-pages long. Stoss took us to the club afterwards and we had a few beers together and then he told me he loved the Army, that he loved the life, but hated being in a basic training regiment. The only reason he'd volunteered for the duty was that promotions were faster. He'd been in Vietnam the year before, was promoted from corporal to buck sergeant and then to staff sergeant and had felt what he was doing was clean compared to what the C.O. here had ordered him to do. Vietnam in 1964. He'd been there before the big buildup. But that was bullshit, too, he said. The advantage was that they left you alone.

Three days later, the letter having achieved nothing except preventing a dishonorable discharge for Niemann, Stoss was 'relieved of duty' in the company and a new buck sergeant named Smith took over our platoon. One of my first published poems is about Niemann:

For Niemann

*(Failed Basic Training, TRO —
Training Required Over)*

You simply weren't cut out for it, snot nose
in the snow, shirt flopping out, entrenching
tool back inside the barracks as we stood
listening to the dogs bark. The SDI, in
your face, yelped, and sent us all, tails
between our legs back up three flights
to help you dress again, load your pack,
clean your M-14, wipe dried muck from your face.

Eight weeks later, we left for advanced schools
and Viet Nam. You stayed, TRO, a second time,
lived another cycle, joined another platoon, waited
for spring in the Ozarks. I have always wondered
why those of us so smart went and you remained
and, if, deep down inside, you laughed.

Smith's moment of truth came in a confrontation with a private in my squad named Mosley. Mosley was the biggest, strongest guy I ever met in the Army: a street kid from East St. Louis who was always in trouble. The first night Smith was in the platoon, we had a push up contest and most of us fagged out early. I think I made it to twenty-five before my arms gave out. When the count got up to 125, Mosely was the only one left. His push ups were uniformly quick, down, up, down, up, no more than a second between the repetitions. We all started counting. "139...150...164...."

Smith was screaming, "You can do it Mosely! 230, the company record! Do it, motherfucker!" "198...210...221...." He never even slowed down, just kept pumping, each repetition as monotonously fast as the previous, his muscles tense and fluid at the same time, up, down, up, down. "227...228...229...."

Mosely pushed himself into the air and held himself there for what seemed like a long, long time. He braced himself on one hand and turned to look at Smith. "Like this motherfucker?" he asked. Smith said, "One more, Mosely, you can do it." Mosely pushed himself up, balanced on one finger and his left foot, then jumped up. "Nah, fuck this shit," he said and walked back to his cot. He was a real son of a bitch, but, goddamnit, he was cool. I wrote a poem for Mosley, too, mostly because we became friends and his night doing push ups has stayed with me all these years:

"Push Ups"

For Mosley
wherever he might be

That night down on the floor
while we counted, your arms,
so fluid, pumped, stretched,
dropped your body an inch above
the tile, then lifted you so high
that something had to give—
the floor, the tiles, the sky—something
had to break. No sweat, just
repetitions, "100," "200," " 229!"

and then you stopped. I knew
why once, the time, the atmosphere,
the need to articulate something
that could not be grunted out
to prove something to yourself

and all of us. Goddamn but you
were cool when you held yourself so still,
looked up at all of us and laughed.

You lifted one hand from the floor, brushed
a drop of sweat from your lip, stood up
and walked away.

We were all in third platoon. Allen Hallmark, who remains a good friend, Mosley, Niemann and I. And we had a reputation for being a real fuck up platoon. At night, we'd laugh at the Army and at the whole Basic Training 'spirit.'

When Stoss left and Smith arrived, things got worse. Matos was always ragging on Third Platoon. We decided we'd show him that we 'could' do it, just preferred not to. Much like Bartleby in that wonderful story by Herman Melville. At final qualification on the rifle range, 3rd platoon, Charley Company, qualified higher than any other platoon in the regiment. That evening, when we were returning from the range, a man in 1st platoon screamed, "3rd Platoon sucks!" Mosely took one swing at him and broke his jaw.

About six weeks into the cycle, Mosley went AWOL. He went home to East St. Louis where he was arrested for stealing a television set. That was actually a good thing, because the MPs came to the squad room to arrest him for beating up one of the NCOs and he had an ideal alibi: he'd been in jail 300 miles from the post.

When he was returned to the platoon by the East St. Louis police, Smith decided that he needed to give a speech. It went something like this:

"I was gonna make Mosley a fuckin' squad leader and what does the son of a bitch do? The motherfucker goes AWOL. I oughta throw the motherfucker out the motherfuckin' window." Mosley stood up and walked over to Smith, stared down at him and then grabbed his wrist in his hand, his own hand dwarfing Smith's. He grinned and said, "We'll see what motherfucker throws what motherfuckin' motherfucker out the motherfuckin' window, motherfucker." He lifted Smith off the floor and held him there by his wrist for a full minute and then lowered him slowly back to the floor. All of 3rd platoon laughed. Smith did not report the incident.

Not much more about Basic. We finished up the cycle, marched, and made E-2. As we were loading up our duffle bags for leave, I dropped by Niemann's room. Stoss had won a pyrrhic victory. Niemann had not received any kind of discharge. TROed again. Only Mosley and I stopped by to wish him luck. I joined Allen and headed back to Texas for two weeks before reporting to Fort George Meade and language training.

Mosley has always served as a kind of symbol for me: some kind of bright intelligence, stunted, trapped inside, denied, replaced with visceral, animal actions. I don't know what happened to him after Basic. I don't know if I want to know.

Believe it or not, I actually kind of enjoyed basic training. I went into it a 200-pound weakling and came out of it a 170-pound weakling, but a whole lot healthier. I made two of the best friends of my life during basic and cemented the friendship over the next several years in language school and then in Vietnam and, finally, in Austin at the University of Texas.

But it all started in Basic where I got to know Allen Hallmark and Don Mohr. We went through a lot, the three of us. After Ft. Leonard Wood, we were sent to Ft. Meade for language school at the Defense Language School (East Coast). A year and a half of being students in an Army thinking only of triple-canopied jungles, of rice paddies, and strange people called VC.

After language school, we went to Goodfellow Air Force Base together and then were sent to Fort Hood, just outside beautiful, dry Killeen, the scum pit of the country where beer was sold only on the post. We trained with the 198th Light Infantry Brigade for mass shipment to Vietnam, cannonfodder helping to form what would become the Americal Division. That's the division that produced Lieutenant William Calley. Hot, dusty days. As tanks rolled by kicking fine dust into the air, we marched.

We spent a half year at Fort Hood and then were loaded onto a train headed west. It was a very long train ride to Oakland, prisoners almost, not allowed off at any of the train's stops. We loaded directly from the train onto the USS Gordon in San Francisco Bay, looking under the bridge to see San Francisco lit up at night, farther away in possibilities than Da Nang, than Chu Lai. Half a life time away now. More than half a life!

Ghost Lights

A still breath on the summer breeze
and high hills in Dak To loom
over us. No quick answers ever
spring to mind, no drops of peace,
not even less than slow, perhaps,
now, inertia, a gradual "settling in."

We no longer even move our lips to ask
or, if we do, old slogans drop from voices
that always have an answer and never find
a truth, just wriggling obfuscations and
something like the Marfa lights dancing
at the dark ends of ancient tunnels.

We transshipped at Da Nang into LSTs. Watched officer-types, blue-eyed, blond, privileged, skiing in Da Nang harbor. Down into the bowels of the landing craft, dark, black, no lights. We sang, shit, folk songs, Baez and Guthrie, spirituals, "Swing low, sweet asshole." We ended with Country Joe and the Fish, leery of going home in boxes. We are not scared, we said to each other. Grunts yell they're gonna kill Charley. Don and Allen and I grin, can almost see ourselves grow nervous, anxious. We are not gonna kill Charley, at least not directly.

The John Wayne bit! Hitting the beaches. Captain tells us we have to stay down; snipers can pick us off if we go topside. Bullshit! Hot and sweaty, nerve-racking. Hundreds and hundreds of teen-aged boys, a few of us older, locked in the dark bowels of the LST, weapons loaded. Old sergeants frantically shouting instructions, last minute advice to a children's crusade bound to end in failure. We hold our weapons at port arms, ready to fire. Yes, no bullshit! Over a thousand of us in cramped quarters, bumping together, banging arms, loading and locking, fumbling with the magazines.

We feel the LST roll onto the beaches. Jeanne Dixon had predicted just two months earlier that Chu Lai would be over-run, everyone killed or POW. Shit! The boats stop, silence. The first crack of light appears thirty feet up at the seam where the massive door meets the deck. We blink in bright light as the ramp moves slowly to the beach. No one is singing. We've seen The Sands of Iwo Jima, Over a thousand boys hold their weapons at port arms, click safeties off.

We run up the ramp, screaming, ready to waste any chickenshit VC waiting on the beach. And we almost fire! We stop. Sergeants yell at us to hold fire. I watch and listen, quiet, as hundreds of sailors, tending the beach at Chu Lai, laugh at us.

A Brief Stay In Chu Lai

A few weeks after we hit the beaches at Chu Lai, I stand in a small hamlet outside the large Army/Marine installation at Chu Lai with a group of techies from the 601st RRU. We are haggling over the cost of this and that, things like genuine onyx chess pieces that would bleed the green right onto your fingers if you were sweating and you were almost always sweating in Chu Lai, Vietnam, Republic of. We stand up above the rice canal that runs behind the small hamlet, all the shops perched precariously on the edge, and haggle for chess men, jackets, genuine Ming vases, and for the rental of female companionship.

I remember clearly a guy from Seattle, Doug something or other, the last name is not important, he is frightened—his first time out of the base camp, though not more than half a klick out—and I think, to cover his fright, he "acts out" the bad guy image—he is not, at heart, a bad guy, just frightened and even more frightened of letting any of us know he is frightened.

Let me describe her for you. She is about four feet tall and cannot be older than twelve—obviously poor, there are no middle class people in Chu Lai, at least not Vietnamese people. She has long brown/black hair and is very slender, breasts just beginning to bud. She carries her baby brother on her hip. But she is clean and her brother is clean. He has on a shirt and, in the way they do things, no bottom. It makes sense. If you're not old enough to go to the bathroom, why not just let the urine and shit fall onto the ground? The girl is tired, has obviously been kept awake by the shelling the night before and has come to the little market for something—fish, vegetables, maybe even to beg from the American long noses she knows will be there.

Let me talk about Doug again. He is also young, filled with American innocence and that kind of tough/naive bravado that is common among 18-year-old American men when they are in groupings of other men near their age or older. He is not, and I want to stress this, he is not a bad person. In Seattle, he had fished and hunted, had played baseball, had dated, had managed somehow to retain his virginity and continued to resent it even the day after the first night he had ever heard the shrill whistle of rockets grow awesomely silent, to be followed by the loud boomings and the cries from men like him but whom he did not know and, now, would never know. Doug is big, right at six feet two inches and burly, with kinky red hair sitting above his normally blotched face. He is not well-educated, but has graduated from high school.

On this day after the night of the rockets, Doug is even worse off than he had been the day before and the day before he had thrown himself under his bunk when the house girl had walked through looking for boots to clean. I mean he is so cherry his face could be used on a box of Smith Brothers cough drops. But on this day, Doug is swaggering. He survived last night. It doesn't matter that almost everyone survived last night. All but three men at the whole, huge base camp had survived last night. Doug had been through his trial by fire and had come out the other end ready to boast about being a man.

I still remember her vividly. No ao dai, just those long silky-looking pants, not new, but with a matching blouse, with worn spots all over it. She didn't have a conical, bamboo hat on, but one of those Australian bush hats that the REMFs had taken to wearing to pretend they actually went out in the bush. The hat's important, you know. Not because it was a hat, but because it was that kind of hat, that kind of bush hat.

You have to understand, too, that Vietnamese women always seemed to look younger than they were or much, much older. Chuyen looked as well developed as some of the prostitutes I would see later in the bars on Tu Do Street in Saigon and along Le Loi Street in Pleiku, but then again, no one really knew how old those prostitutes were. So when Doug saw Chuyen he saw more than a young girl holding her baby brother, he saw more than a child holding another child and he was scared in spite of the bullshit and he was embarrassed to be the only one, he thought, in the whole detachment not to have found some woman to "make him a man" when he was still in the States and, be assured, that's how Doug thought of it, of sex, of releasing into a vagina instead of into a handkerchief. He saw Chuyen and began to walk toward her.

"How much?" he asked.

"Tôi không bíêt," she said.

"I said 'how much?' you whore!" Doug screamed.

"I no whore," she said.

"How the fuck much?" he asked again and grabbed at her shoulders.

"Di di mau, G.I. I no whore," Chuyen said again.

That's pretty close to the whole conversation. It didn't get really bad until we all started laughing. "Hey, Doug," someone screamed, I don't know who, not me. "Hey, Doug, CherryBoy! Can't even buy it!" "Show her your money," someone else screamed at him.

The whole group roared, laughed, tormented him.

Doug's face turned an even deeper red and he grabbed Chuyen hard and pulled her towards him. Chuyen spat in his face and Ngo began crying.

"Sonofabitch!" Doug screamed in her face and pushed her hard. Chuyen and her baby brother fell to the ground.

I was, as is so often the case, the oldest person in the group, a Spec 4 linguist who would rather have been anywhere else. With help, I managed to grab Doug and shove him back to the diddeyboppers and calm Chuyen down. It always amazed me that just the fact that I could speak the language a little could make some Vietnamese people want to listen and trust. I don't mean speak the patois that most Americans could speak, but actually converse in Vietnamese.

A true story: anticlimactic, certainly. If I were doing it as fiction, it would certainly not have ended this way. I mean I assume Doug's still alive somewhere. I don't know, though, about Chuyen and Ngo. True stories are often as sad as fiction and we don't always find out how they end.

I can't imagine why all that comes back to memory. I suspect the cultural differences, the way so many of us treated so many of the Vietnamese, played a larger part than many of us imagine in our failure to win the "hearts and minds" of the Vietnamese people.

Snapshots On the Road To Peace

Pleiku, Vietnam in the Central Highlands

I am sitting on a hill just a few klicks east of Pleiku (Po Lei Ku being Jarai Montagnard for "Big Town"). Snapshot: In front of me, a dozen Vietnamese women are squatting, washing GI clothing in aluminum wash basins. Each woman has her own basin, each one squats in a way that I cannot imitate for more than a few minutes at a time. From the hilltop, I can look down at the city to the east and on past it to what we all called Titty Mountain…two high hills side by side with the Fourth Division nestled at the base. The area is like a beehive. Airplanes and choppers buzzing in and out. At night, from the same vantage point, just outside my hootch, I can often see Snoopy (AKA Puff) raining machine gun fire in red rivulets down upon what they must think is a Viet Cong emplacement.

Not today. This is my first week in Pleiku and what I see is a red tornado, a dust devil from the bare hill that has been stripped clean of vegetation before I got there. I suspect it was defoliated by Agent Orange but have no real way of knowing. The dust devil races, almost alive, through the area where the women are working and carry their wash pans into the sky before dropping them not far away. The women start over. I have walked right through these mini-tornadoes and left with my pockets filled with red sand and with grit all over me.

I take a TriLambretta (5 dong = 5 cents) into Pleiku and stop at a schoolhouse on Le Loi Street. I look over the short stone fence into the schoolyard and see children playing on the crumbled ruins of a Buddha that must have been at least ten feet tall before it was bombed and shattered. Years later, I write a poem about it and about the children. I never saw the Buddha when it was whole, but did chat with a couple of the kids. They enjoyed playing on the fragments, tossing them at each other. I catch one of the tiny missiles and sit down and chat with one of the boys. He is about 11 years old and is smoking a Salem cigarette. Cheerful, grinning, he warns me about sitting on the Buddha's hand. I am more astonished by his managing to stay cheerful than he is about my speaking his language.

Father Buddha

I walked two klicks down Le Loi Street
to a school yard, a buddha broken in the dust
shattered by a rocket meant for us,
and saw you sitting in his hand
tossing carved pieces of the statue's feet,
not even caring where they'd land.

What mattered was that I did not want to be
where and what I was and saw
that you had also had no choice. Some law,
legal in my case, chance in yours,
with no way out that you or I could see,
gave me a twelve-month, you a lifetime, tour.

We shared a cigarette and watched the smoke
rise into the red dust Pleiku air.
You grinned, blew smoke rings with the flair
that comes only when you're very young.
You told me I was on the Buddha's throat
and should beware the Buddha's tongue.

I remember that once, when the war was calm,
we laughed and played with shattered stone,
and know there can be no way to atone
for all the wounds, the pain, the death.
If you still live, rest quietly in Father Buddha's palm;
if not, sleep peacefully in the Buddha's breath.

A short distance down Le Loi Street (Highway 14 leading to Dak To and Kon Tum to the north and Ban Me Thuot to the South—this is all Montagnard country, though not all Jarai) I come to one of my favorite places in Pleiku: Sông, Vietnamese for "life" and for "river." A young man, for some reason not in the Army of the Republic of Vietnam (ARVN), paints what the American soldiers most frequently want to purchase: black velvet paintings with women in ao dais or children on water buffalo or various Elvis poses. In the back, he has his own art, paintings of Pleiku...the war, children, women, but art…not tourist stuff. During the Tet Offensive, he and his shop disappear. Why I loved the place so much: the artist was an artist and his shop, when you got past the stuff he did over and over for so many American soldiers, was what Vietnam could have, should have been.

The children you do not want to see: They are barefoot, oddly cheerful. Some have suppurating wounds with dirty bandages, one has no right foot, another has scars across her face from shrapnel. I have a wonderful photo of one young girl carrying her crying younger brother. Snapshot: another boy, holding his younger brother, staring into the entrance of a Buddhist shrine. It is a rare moment of peace.

Soldiers near a small pizza parlor on a side street off Le Loi. They have surrounded three women, all prostitutes. The photo: a small boy in baggy pants walks by a sign saying "Pizza Italian Style 500 Dong"…three soldiers with M-16s have women wrapped in their arms, the women wearing tight pants and tops, saying things like "I love you so much only 500 Dong"…same price as the pizza, about five dollars. "I love you all night, GI, only ten dolla." Everything is cheap.

I am sitting on a bunker. A movie is playing behind me, any of a number of B grade movies, maybe cowboys and Indians. Or I am inside the club and listening to a Filipino rock band, on tour, with strippers. They are singing "I gotta get outta this place / if it's the last thing I ever do…." The women are stripping, down to nothing, making kissy faces at the GIs. I go back out and sit on the bunker. I hear the shrill sound of a rocket and then another. No one leaves the club. I hear the music through the doors and watch as the rockets fly overhead, hear the shrill sounds stop, then see flashes of the explosions as they hit the large Air Force base down in the valley. The whole time I am in Vietnam, we are mortared only three times. I get a small scratch on one of my toes one October night…that's it. I don't report it, don't want a purple heart for a tiny cut on my big toe.

That's enough snapshots for now. When I go to Pleiku, either hitch or take a TriLam, I attract small crowds. That's because I usually sit in an open air restaurant and read Nhan Dan (Citizen/ People) newspaper. The people who surround me are not terribly surprised that I can speak their language, but they are impressed that I can read it. They always ask me to read aloud to them. I am almost as surprised as they are that I know their language fairly well. I've mentioned this before, but the real test for me is being able to function conversationally in a group, not just one on one. I am able to do that after a month in Vietnam.

The first month I am in Pleiku, three of my linguist friends and I start a small school to teach English to teens in Pleiku. If they can speak English, they can get civilian draft-exempt jobs working for the Army or Air Force. We have ten students. Le-Linh, Son, Bao… and others whose names have left me after 30 years.

For My Students In Vietnam

The English class at Lake Bien Ho
laughs, shouts, sings Christmas carols
in broken English, sing-songy, tonal
inflections, music that does not, somehow,
fit in this warm, green land. A small boy
talks about the Buddha. Not long ago
a bonze kindled himself in Saigon, burned
with intensity, no screams, a desperate
song, silence fell on a noisy city.

At Lake Bien Ho the teachers
have brought a Christmas tree, presents
for their students: books, candles,
cakes and candy. They sit on the bank
and sing of shepherds and their flocks.
An old man on a water buffalo watches.

I do not see any of them again after the Tet Offensive.

Some background photos

People who know me will hardly recognize this picture. I am STRAC! Clean shaven, short hair, starched uniform and I am more physically fit than I have ever been in my life. Want to lose weight? Go through basic training and then train for six months in the hot Texas sun before shipping to a war zone. The pounds peel off like juicy orange peels. That was me: dress greens, Spec 4 rank insignia, overseas cap. Second shot: I am on top of a bunker in messy fatigues. I am wearing a flak jacket and pisspot (steel helmet) plus baseball-style green cap. I am holding the trigger of a 50 caliber machine gun and aiming it out past a cleared zone into low-level jungle.

And a third shot: I am standing near the bunker just outside my hootch. I am wearing civilian clothes and have a pewter peace symbol hanging around my neck. All my soldier friends in Vietnam wear them.

These snapshots are from the 1967 – 1968 Vietnam War year and they are all me. The 1967 – 1968 war year. That was a helluva year for the war. It began for me in Pleiku when we were mortared early in September. I was not wounded, but heard pieces of shrapnel rattle through the hootch I shared with one of my good friends, Allen Hallmark, and other linguist friends I have lost touch with: Jim Brow, Will Chapman, Richard Miller and a few others.

Later that month, I was sent with Jim to Dak To for two weeks. That was just after the largest battle up until that time of the entire war. The battle was fought around Dak To, mostly on Hill 875, only a few klicks away from the triborder area (the area where Kampuchea, Laos and Vietnam come together in the foothills of the Annamese Cordillera) And then, sitting on my hill in Pleiku as the Tet Offensive played out around me and seeing it all end, not in person, but by television and radio at Khe Sanh. Some of you may not realize this, and I am not the first person to say it, but we won all the battles during the Tet Offensive and lost the whole damned war at the same time. When LBJ resigned and Nixon was elected, we should have just left and saved the lives of more than 20,000 Americans who would still die in that little war and untold hundreds of Vietnamese.

I am at Lake Bien Ho, Peace Lake, which lies about halfway between Engineer Hill (home of the 555th Combat Engineers) where I live and work and Pleiku City. The lake is mostly a Vietnamese place. Americans just don't go there. The first time I visited, I was somewhat frightened: perhaps the VC would capture me. After that time, though, I felt comfortable. I am in civilian clothes wearing my peace symbol. A small boy comes up to me and asks me for a cigarette. His mother pulls him away and says, "Khong phai, khong cai nay…" "No, not in this place." The lake is peaceful, somehow separate from the war. I visit it several times before the Tet Offensive, not once afterwards. Afterwards, anyone leaving the hill was required to wear a uniform and carry an M-16. I lean against a tree and think of Thoreau and Walden. Do not get me wrong. I am sure that in Thoreau's day Walden Pond was much more tranquil than is Peace Lake, but for me, during those months, there were some very clear depths to be explored, issues to be resolved.

Sitting in the market along Le Loi Street. Flies buzzing around fairly fresh fish. Vegetables baking in the sun. Old women with teeth black from chewing betel nuts shooing the flies away as if it did not matter that they would come right back. A friend of mine is scoring grass out on the street. We'll smoke in the bunker by candle light later tonight.

A short way away, a tall Montagnard man is leaning over a fire lighting a hand-rolled cigarette. He wears nothing but a dirty loin cloth. His wife is bare-breasted. The Vietnamese women laugh at them. He has more dignity than most of us squatting and sitting in the market.

Before going back to the hill, I walk to the end of Le Loi Street and into a small tea shop. The old Vietnamese woman who runs the place serves hot tea with poppy blossoms floating on top and seed in the bottom. We drink the green tea and she talks about unimportant things. It is a rare luxury to speak of unimportant things. Walking back down Le Loi Street, I notice that most of the more prosperous shops are owned by Indians and, after 5 p.m., when most of the GIs return to their bases, they lock the store fronts with chain link. I see that today in some neighborhoods in San Antonio but do not recall having seen it back in the early 60s when I was living in Southeast Texas and driving 20 miles every week day to teach at Silsbee High School.

Helicopters were how we got around in Vietnam. When Jim and I went to Dak To, back in September, 1967, the battle just ended but the base camp being rocketed and mortared almost every other night, I sat on the floor of the HUEY, legs dangling over the side, and watched the hills and mountains roll by under me. I could see hundreds of bomb craters, many filled with water. If you have read Tim O'Brien's Going After Cacciato, these are the same kinds of bomb craters that Cacciato fishes in. And they are everywhere until the chopper finally begins to fly over triple canopy jungle and we can no longer see the ground.

I have been "in country" for a few months and have been in a mortar attack once, but, as the HUEY lands at Dak To, for the very first time, I feel that I am in a war zone. Now, for the first time, I see soldiers who look like they have been in a fight. I am living for a few weeks in a small tent and from time to time see LRRPs walking into the camp. LRRPs: long range reconnaissance patrols, small teams of 5 – 7 men who are dropped deep in the jungles to try to locate concentrations of enemy troops. I have immense respect for their courage and, at the same time, doubt their sanity. They hang together, do not talk much to other people.

I have told this story often. I suppose I have obsessed over it a bit. And I know, rationally, that I am not truly the responsible person. I did not give the order and I did not pull the trigger. And Bao might not even have died. I am in a small valley in Kontum Province, not far from the very small town of Dak To. I have been in Dak To twice. It's not very impressive…mostly, from what I see, the town now exists only as a supplier to the Americans: soft drinks, prostitutes, laundries. Most of the soldiers I am with at Dak To are from the 4th Division and from the 101st Screaming Eagles (the same division featured in the Spielberg/Hanks production of Stephen Ambrose's *Band of Brothers*, no longer strictly paratroopers, but now air mobile, like the 1st Air Cav…they ride to war in helicopters instead of jumping from the sky). On days when the camp sends convoys to Pleiku, someone in the surrounding hills reports on the composition of the convoys.

The reason Jim and I were sent to Dak To was to locate the VC who was sending the reports. It wasn't difficult to do. We knew he was close by because the reports came over the air almost as soon as the convoys left the camp. They were always signed "Bao." That could have been his name or could have simply signified that he was reporting, since bao is a vietnamese word meaning "to report" as well as a name. We triangulated his signal and notified the commander when he was up.

One morning in the war, I told the colonel that Bao was broadcasting and within minutes saw jets flying over the hill he was on and seconds later saw the bursts of fiery blossoms of napalm cover the side of the hill. I have always assumed that Bao died at that moment and that I was responsible. I am at least as responsible as the Colonel and as the jet jockey who dropped the napalm. A week later, someone else was up, reporting on convoys leaving Dak To. That was, I suppose, a kind of beginning to the journey. Perhaps "journey" is too strong a word, it bears too many connotations of some kind of exemplary pilgrimage and it is not.

A few photos not related to much of anything

I am chatting with my hootchmaid. Her job is to keep the hootch clean, polish boots, clean clean clean…almost anything except our rifles. I am trying to improve my Vietnamese by learning the Vietnamese word for marijuana. I know it is a leaf, so assume the word starts with "thuoc la." I check the word for tobacco in my dictionary—a dictionary that does not contain some of the more important words in the language—and that doesn't work either. So, I begin fabricating, trying to come up with the word or phrase. I say, "Thuoc…" and mime smoking and holding the smoke deep inside. Finally, I locate some form of inspiration and combine "thuoc la" with "can xa" (a phrase meaning "to see far"). I like the rhyme though I am growing increasingly frustrated. When I combine those words, she frowns and informs me that I do not want "thuoc la can xa."

The next day, she brings me a small glass cylinder containing a dark brown liquid. "Thuoc la can xa," she says, and hands it to me. I have no idea what is in the little cylinder, possibly heroin or opium, certainly not grass. I pay her five dollars American and wind up dropping the stuff down in the latrine. I have friends who would have tried it without knowing what it was. I have never been quite that brave…or foolish. Again, fluency means different things to different people.

On my hill, the hill I share with approximately 300 other Americans, there is a berm scooped up by the Engineers and completely encircling all of us. Every thirty or so yards, there is a bunker, perhaps seven feet high, with a small rain shelter on top. The bunker is sandbagged all the way up, the sandbags covering ConEx containers that brought munitions from the world. Some of the sandbag have split open and red dust has trickled down to paint the sides of the bunker. Two men sleep inside the ConEx bunker while the third stands on top of the bunker.

On guard duty, I have one 50 caliber machine gun, one M-60 machine gun (loaded with UN consistent bullets), one M-79 grenade launcher, switches to the five Claymores in front of the bunker and facing out. I have checked those earlier. There is a little message printed on one side that says, "This side faces enemy." I arm the claymores with a detonating device then climb back on top of the bunker. Most evenings pass quietly. Other evenings, I see something very much like a war movie: red flares, gunships responding, firing, amber flares shot into the air by the artillery and drifting down below parachutes. But, mostly, no entertainment is provided.

The berm. I visit frequently, even while not on guard duty. On Christmas Eve, 1967, I take a fifth of Ruffino's Chianti out to the berm and lie down, facing the perimeter. You can see fairly clearly about fifty yards out. The engineers have installed powerful floodlights all around the perimeter to enable us to see and to blind any possible VC who might try to sneak in. I drink to the engineers. And I drink again, old Eben Flood having nothing on me. I whisper Yeats's "Innisfree" and the great opening stanzas on Eliot's "Love Song of J. Alfred Prufrock." I dredge up every line of any poem I can about leaving, about going somewhere. And, with each poem, I take an-other swallow of Chianti. "Let us go then, you and I…," "I will arise and go now…," "Two roads diverge in a yellow wood," and on and on and on, adding the walking song from The Lord of the Rings ("The road goes ever on and on…") for good measure. I get incredibly drunk. And I am by myself in the dark and getting noisier and noisier. I do not pass out, but eventually rant and rave so loudly that my friends carry me back to my hootch and put me to bed.

Ce n'est pas merde! A starry, starry night. I am standing on top of a bunker on Engineer Hill (HQ of the 555th Engineers and of the 330th RRC) about a mile from the big Air Force Base in Pleiku.

Quiet night: no mortars, no rockets. No show of any kind. Boring. Sometimes on guard duty, I am able to listen to rockets fly over us and watch the explosions as they land in and around the AFB, but not this night. Nothing is happening tonight. I am wearing normal go out to the bunkers and guard the perimeter stuff: fatigues, flak jacket, boots. I have my M-16 with me. And I have already checked the claymores to make sure they are pointed the right way and checked the long belt of 50 caliber ammo to make sure things look right (and how would I know? I've never fired the thing). The two M-60s (which I have fired and qualified expert on) and the M-79 (which I have fired twice) are ready to go in case the boredom is broken by something I can shoot at. Oh, yes, the other two guys I share guard duty with tonight are in the bunker sleeping.

The boredom is broken, but not by anything I can fire a weapon at. A horde of wasps has attacked. Back in the States I know wasps do not swarm like bees and certainly not at night. But these are VC wasps and feel the night belongs to them. Ugly critters. Within a few seconds, they have taken over the whole top of the bunker. Why? Because I desert my post. I jump off the side of the bunker at the first sting. I know I can guard the perimeter just as well from the bottom of the damned thing. Besides, no one except these wasps have ever attacked us.

I go inside and call the OD (Officer of the Day? Why does he work at night?) to report enemy aerial infiltration and he refuses to believe me. I invite him to come down and take a look. He orders me back up to the top of the bunker and I tell him I will be happy to follow him. He drives his jeep down to the bunker and, while he does not exactly say, "Follow me!" does climb halfway up the ladder before being stung. "As you were," he says and leaves.

So, that's the story. One night in the war, my bunker was overrun by the VC Air Force and I shamelessly surrendered to superior forces.

Back on the Hill

After Dak To, things were very quiet up on the hill for several months. Just a few images, None terribly war-like.

In mid November, the VC mortar the hill again. I am sitting in my hootch, reading, drinking, doing nothing much in particular. * CLICK * Olive drab boxer shorts, flat belly (well flatter than it has been since). I am probably reading *Ramparts* to which I subscribe or I might have been reading Thomas Hardy (I read all of his novels and poems while in Vietnam). I was able to check them out from the Air Force library down at the base. I hear the thumping sound from outside, hear the sound of shrapnel in the hootch, pinging against the lockers, smacking down on the concrete floor. I do what any sensible soldier would do: hide under the bed until the barrage stops. That sounds a bit more cowardly than it is. The cot has a piece of ¾ inch plywood between the mattress and the springs. The shrapnel would have a hard time getting through it. When the mortar fire stops, I put on my helmet and grab my M-16 and race, half-naked out to the berm. Nothing happens. No attack, no sappers, nothing. Oh, two things happen: 1. My big toe is bleeding and 2. I smoke a cigarette. The first is irrelevant; the second is a bad habit that I continue to practice until June 6, 2001.

Snapshot: Guy goes out the gates. Doesn't come back. He's an analyst, one of the guys who takes all the translations and tries to make sense out of the mess. He shows up later that same night: outside our perimeter with his M-16. He points it in toward the berm and starts yelling, pointing it at our bunkers. It is dark. Artillery fires an illumination round that drifts downward on its parachute. We see our analyst: totally naked with his pisspot and rifle. One of our sergeants, and I have too conveniently forgotten the names of all the sergeants in the 330th, talks him back into camp.

We lose him for a week (under examination by the shrinks) and then he comes back to work. He is much admired by everyone. I have never really understood why he did what he did. We had it pretty easy for the most part. I don't think anyone except Americans ever fired a gun inside our perimeter and no one ever fired at us from outside the perimeter. I suspect the people most likely to have some kind of anxiety attack…whatever it should be called…or those who just stayed on the hill all the time, those people who never went downtown to Pleiku. I don't know and won't know.

And another: The club at night. Boys playing together… gambling, drinking, making wild claims. Viet-Nam veterans will remember piss tubes. Tubes stuck into the ground, the openings covered with thick screen. One guy, on a dare, licks them all clean. He wins $25 in MPC. Boys playing together. Gross out contests. I gross out fairly easily and don't participate. Xuan and Xuan work in the Club. That's a pretty common name for Vietnamese women, means "Spring." Xuan 1 is beautiful; Xuan 2 is a bit chunky. Both undergo an almost constant siege from the men. Almost everyone wants to get Xuan 1 into bed; the rest are willing to settle for Xuan 2. As far as I can tell, no one ever succeeded with Xuan 1.

Bunker shot: Just outside our hootch is a deep bunker. It was dug out by the engineers with their heavy equipment and sandbagged by us. It has thick beams across the top and sandbags go all the way up the sides and across the roof. There are rifle slots like you see in some medieval castles. It is well-lighted within: successions of candles on chianti bottles, various colors of wax dripping down the sides. We have a boombox in the bunker, an extension cord leads from the hootch to a small half height refrigerator, stocked with beer. We are REMFs: there is no real reason to be uncomfortable. We rarely smoke grass inside the bunker, but do sit on top of it from time to time for a companionable smoke. The bunker is a kind of social club. We gather there, drink cold beer and talk about the war and music and what's happening back in the world. Not often, not often, but occasionally.

Meanwhile, back in the war: By Christmas we have begun receiving more and more messages from more and more parts of the country. Message after message warns people to prepare, message after message mentions a "general uprising." We write a major report in January stating that there is a strong likelihood of a general attacks all over SVN at the end of January. It is ignored. General Westmoreland predicts that the war will be over soon, that the enemy is unable to mount a major attack anywhere in the country. We continue to do our job.

Christmas. I don't want to write about Christmas. Here is a little poem instead. I wrote this years after the war, when we were engaged in yet another, faster war. The Persian Gulf War, Desert Storm, made many of us who had been in Vietnam begin to think about our own war again. And I am writing this as the World Trade Center and the Pentagon have been viciously attacked by terrorists. I suspect that most of us who have been in wars flash back a bit, whether we have PTSD or not, upon our own wars. I have written about Christmas in Vietnam before, during the first Persian Gulf War. That is enough.

Christmas, 1967

The sand bags look the same:
a dismal green-grey bag leaks red clay
upon the bags below. Outside the perimeter
children pick though the garbage,
thrown out waste of a thousand men.
Christmas in Pleiku, 1967, war fills
the surrounding hills. Across the valley
we see cloud puffs of artillery and

at night red, green, amber flares dangle,
shining bright beneath white parachutes:
displays in sound and light
rivaling the staged events of a thousand
towns across the "world" on New Year's Day.
But this is Christmas: a time of truce.

Snapshots of Tet, 1968

In those months between Dak To and Tet, my own time *d'entre deux guerre*, I suppose, I see a few guns fired in anger, but none on the hill where I live. I see the Air Force base down in the valley get rocketed a few more times. I see wounded children and I mean physically as well as mentally. But most of the children I see and meet are amazingly cheerful. I mean they are not having what you and I would call a normal childhood: "Hey, G.I., you buy cigarettes me! Hey, G.I., you give me 100 p? Hey, G.I., you want boom boom?!!! I take you girl so fine… only 14…guarantee virgin!" Kids. Gotta love 'em. That's Pleiku, my friends. The corner of 14th and 19th streets.

For months, things seem fine. Very quiet. No major attacks have happened since Dak To. Some people organize a "don't eat Thanksgiving turkey boycott for peace" right there in country and a few people deliberately do not eat turkey on that day. I am personally amazed at the logistical supply tunnel that can provide so many fat turkeys so many thousands of miles from home. I am for peace in some kind of vague as yet undefinable way, but eat turkey and stuffing anyway. What the hell! The damned turkeys are already dead and I am never terribly militant about some things. Christmas comes and goes and, amazingly, there are very few violations of the Christmas truce.

Snapshot: Our operations area is a large tent, olive drab with a wooden floor and big fans blowing the dust around. When we want to cool off, there are air-conditioned areas dealing with things we have no need to know but we don't care and neither do the people who do have a need to know. Otherwise, when not working, we play…at the lake, in the club, in Pleiku…or we teach our students who learn so quickly. And we translate messages and the cryppies break codes and there is much I will not be able to say for decades about what we are doing. NOT, I assure you because the same codes are being used today. If they are, some dirty ratfink commie's head should be rolling, but because we have sworn we will not talk about it.

I read *Stars & Stripes*, have *Newsweek* delivered, get the *Beaumont Enterprise*, read the Vietnamese language local rags. Everything I read promises me that the VC are on the run. And, yes, ma'am,

General William C. Westmoreland himself assures the President, the troops and the whole by god damned world that the VC will never be able to conduct a large-scale battle again. This was in mid-January and two weeks later… Well, two weeks later at just about midnight, I sit on top of my bunker. Yes, the one with the Ruffino's Chianti bottles, wicker wrapped around the base, candles of varying colors having dripped their wax down in Jackson Pollock style. That bunker. I sit on top of it and listen to the radio. I do not see, but feel hundreds of soldiers walking past us, dividing in lines around the Hill and marching down into the valley, skirting the Air Force base, moving, silently, slowly, in a well-organized display of military skill into the town of Pleiku. No one sees them, it is only conjecture that that is one of the routes the two National Liberation Front regiments travel to get into Pleiku.

What I do know is that I listen to the movement on the radio, hear individual voices speaking to other voices, hear people describe the terrain they are on. Inside our Ops area people are faithfully transcribing what I am hearing and are passing it on. I do not know precisely where the VC are. Finally, though, I hear the sound of a huge firefight, see tracers…green for the bad guys, red for us good guys. I always thought it was very convenient that our tracers glowed red and theirs glowed green. I see and hear explosions down in the city…dark night…flashing lights. In the east and west, amber flares shoot up in an explosion of artillery and drift down on parachutes. We are alerted … sent to the perimeter, poised to return fire that never comes. The Tet Offensive of 1968 is not about American bases; it is an attempt to take control of all the major cities in the South and, in direct disobedience to General William C. Westmoreland, the VC demonstrate that they can, indeed, wage war all across the country on the same very freaking night!!!

Two days. That's how long they stay in Pleiku. Two days. They kill a number of people, we kill a number of people. They ignore a number of people for some reason we cannot explain. The province chief and the mayor? Hey, they aren't in Pleiku right now. They left town a few days before Tet for a big party in Saigon. Xuans 1 and 2? Our very own bar girls? For some reason, they, the barber, the hootch girls, all the Mess Hall help...none reports to work that day. Such an epidemic of flu you have never seen!

Here is a news flash: We Americans and out ARVN allies win the Tet Offensive and achieve something that Westmoreland had claimed precipitously: the VC had become an ineffective fighting force. From Tet on, most battles would be fought by NVA forces from the North. Oh, yes, we also lost the war during those few days while winning all the battles.

Some people blame the media. When did we lose the war, daddy? When Uncle Walter Cronkite reacted badly to the Tet Offensive and to the false words the generals had been spreading for a long time. It was not, though, Walter Cronkite and the "leftist" media that lost the war or caused Americans to lose the will to wage the war. It was the generals who had ignored their own intelligence reports and had consistently lied to the American people. We kept on fighting a war we had lost in 1968 for five more years and suffered 20,000+ more American and untold numbers of Vietnamese deaths.

Snapshot of the Aftermath: For some weeks, I am not allowed back in town and then only if I am wearing my fatigues, a flak jacket and helmet. And...if I carry my M-16. What I do is mope. I confess. My own little war has been ruined. It isn't fun anymore. My school is closed and I never see my students again though I hear that Son got a job with the Air Force. I sit on top of my bunker and get drunk. More than once. I am getting drunk much too often. A year or two later, I stop drinking altogether. I decide not to become an alcoholic. The siege at Khe Sanh is still going on. I watch the rest of it from Washington, D.C., on television. I get out of Viet-Nam before the seige ends. Ends? The bad guys leave. Then we leave and they come back. It's that kind of war.

A few (very few) thoughts: My own war has been a fairly peaceful war. No one has actually shot at me. I've suffered from a mild cut on my toe (a band-aid fixed that). I have a few interesting moments when I know a mortar could land in such a way that it might kill me. And I have been scared close to death while trying to bury myself face down on a concrete floor. But...few people had easier 365-day tours than I had.

And so, I don't have a good answer to Marianne's questions. But I could answer it this way: I got to know a lot of people in Vietnam and not just American soldiers. My students were wonderful young

Vietnamese in their late teens and they deserved to live in a country that was not at war. I suspect many of them went through "reeducation" camps, but know that is better than their being maimed or killed. I saw too many people missing limbs. Heard of too many deaths, not just American deaths. But, most importantly, I never heard a good reason why we were there in the first place.

There were official explanations: we were invited in to help a struggling country retain a democratic form of government. But it never seemed very democratic to me and most of the people who lived there didn't seem to care whether a South Vietnamese president like Diem or Thieu or Ky or a North Vietnamese communist like Chairman Ho led them. We were keeping the communists from world dominion. They didn't dominate the world even after we withdrew from Viet-Nam and the other dominoes somehow refused to fall. I guess, ultimately, the real reason is that the whole thing never seemed to make much sense to me. And, if we are going to go to war, the reasons ought to make sense.

When I returned from Viet-Nam, I joined a group called GIs United Against the War and began to march, first in Fayetteville, North Carolina, and later in the big anti-war parades in Washington, D.C. I did get back to Austin and completed work on my Ph.D. in English and continued to march, this time on Guadalupe Street. Five years after I returned from Viet-Nam, we finally left that sad country and a few years later, northern tanks rolled into Saigon. There are photos I did not take but that are seared into my memory: helicopters leaving the American embassy, thousands of Vietnamese mobbing the embassy to try to get out, a young girl burning with napalm, General Loan executing a VC. These all add up and are all a part of that road to peace.

Leaving Vietnam

A night in a cheap bar. Nha Trang, South Vietnam. I am drinking ba-muoi-ba and talking with a young lady who says her name is Thich Duong Dang. I call her Dang (pronounced Zang in Vietnamese). She wants me to buy her a drink, but I know the drink will be very expensive tea with just enough alcohol in it to make it smell like "a drink." You see, Dang is a bar girl, maybe 19 or 20 years old, five years younger than I am. What money she earns she gets from having American GIs buy alcoholic beverages for her, hoping she'll go to bed with them, but she will not and she is paid by the bar management based upon the number of expensive, watered down drinks she can sell.

I get the impression she is enjoying herself. Her normal clientele cannot speak Vietnamese and she normally has to talk in some kind of pidgin that resembles baby talk with them. We, on the other hand, can discuss the war, poetry, art, whatever we like, simply because I can speak in her language. I would like to get something straight: I am not at the Doc Lap Bar for the purpose of leasing female companionship for the evening. Tomorrow, I am leaving Vietnam. I'll take a short flight down to Cam Ranh Bay and board what we have come to call a "Freedom Bird" back to the United States. I am in the Independence Bar ("doc lap" means "independence" in Vietnamese) to have a few beers, my last drop of "33" beer ("ba muoi ba" means "33" in Vietnamese) before leaving country. Dang rubs the front of my leg with her foot as we talk...about Yeats as I recall. I have just done an execrable translation "The Lake Isle of Innisfree" into Vietnamese for her sake and she does not like all this talk of rising up and going to a wee small island.

Dang is, and there is not another word for it, exceptionally beautiful. She wears a deep purple ao dai and white silk pants that fit tight around her ass and then flows out from her ankles. Her skin is flawless and she has not had that operation that some Vietnamese prostitutes get to make their eyes look more western. She is slender, with a small waist and bust that gravity has not yet had time to play with and that, I suspect, nothing else has ever played with. She is not really a prostitute, only a bar girl, and that is, if anything, a less honest profession.

In spite of curfews in Nha Trang, the Doc Lap never really closes; the bartender only turns the light inside down and the lights outside off. The imitation American rock band from Manilla does a heavy, syrupy version of "We gotta get outta this place / if it's the last thing we ever do..." and seques into "Feeling Groovy." Dang and I chat quietly. She invites me to her house for the evening.

"Much too dangerous for an American to go back to base so late at night." She kisses me on the cheek, "Plus, I want to talk some more." I give her 10,000 Dong (a little less than $10) to buy a bottle of Scotch and, at her suggestion, will meet her outside so no one will see her leave with an American. Now, I am not stupid. I know that as soon as she goes through the door she will vanish for the evening. After all, I've already told her I'm leaving Viet-Nam tomorrow. Actually, this morning, it's already after midnight.

The bartender laughs at me and tells me she is still a virgin and that I have wasted my money on her. But if I want a woman for the night, he has the prettiest in Vietnam, "Ah, choi oi!, dep lam!" I laugh back and tell him I want no other woman than Dang. When I get out into the narrow street in front of the bar, it's so dark I can hardly make out the road. This part of Nha Trang is filled with two-story buildings hanging over narrow streets and it reminds me of nothing more than a poor, older area of San Antonio that has not yet been gentrified.

"Hey, GI! You looking for Dang?" A young boy on a bicycle. I squint my eyes and look at him.

"Yeh, we were having a little talk."

"You come with me, GI."

I follow him for twenty or so blocks through the dark streets of the city the French had called (if I remember correctly) Touraine. Nha Trang has been one of my favorite cities since I arrived in Vietnam a year earlier. A coastal resort city during the French colonial period, its French architecture has hardly suffered during the years of war and the beaches along that section of the South China Sea are wonderful. But Nha Trang has changed since the Tet Offensive of 1968. It's a spookier place late at night and the young boy and I seem to be the only two people on the street. The young boy. He seems about 12 years old and I assume Dang has asked him to show me the way to her home. So, I follow him.

When we get to the house, the boy points to a stairway on the outside leading up to the second floor. "You wait for me," I say.

When I knock on the door, Dang opens it. Wearing flannel PJs and looking as if she has just climbed out of the shower, she is obviously surprised to see me. I laugh and say "Surprise!" Her response puzzles me. I would have expected almost any reaction from mild amusement to frigid hostility, what I see is fear.

She looks down the stairs and sees the boy grinning up at her. Her dark eyes fasten on mine and she whispers, "Xin anh di (please go)."

"Tai sao? (Why?)," I ask. And she explains how being seen with an American could hurt her reputation so much that she might have to become a prostitute just to survive. I leave. As I said, I am not looking for leased sex, but I had enjoyed the conversation at the Doc Lap. I hope she got along okay after I left Nha Trang and Vietnam, but have no way of knowing.

When I get back down the stairs, I tell the boy to take me to a house where it is safe for Americans to sleep and he leads me another 15 or more blocks through the narrow streets of old Touraine. I knock on the door of a small house and an older woman answers. "All girls in use," she says. "I don't need a girl, just a place to sleep," I tell her. She nods and I pay the boy 1,000 dong for his assistance and go into the house. The woman leads me to a narrow cot in the middle of a small room that has ten narrow beds surrounded by scrim-like material, cloth you can see through. All of the beds are occupied and some of the Americans are still getting their money's worth from the women they have paid. Not a pretty sight. And the sounds are worse.

I nod to the woman, give her ten dollars and lie down on the cot. Almost immediately, a girl who can not be more than 12 or 13 climbs into the bed with me. "You fuck me, GI? Only ten dollars." I get up immediately and pull her out of the bed. I give her ten dollars and tell her to go to sleep somewhere. And then, with the sound of working women and men fucking, I fall asleep.

The next morning, when I get on the plane, I think I am leaving Vietnam forever, but I don't believe anyone who was there ever really leaves, not all the way.

Why I Still Write About the War

I can sometimes move forward without writing about Vietnam in my journal and then something brings it back to me: the way the water looks in the Laguna Madre, a cool breeze on campus, catching the silhouette of a telephone pole above the woods in my backyard late at night and mistaking it for a giant bird with a huge beak, the smell of peanut butter cookies in the oven, almost anything if it hits at just the right moment.

Almost it is as if someone turned a switch to the ON position and words begin to flow. Not always good words, not always the right words, but words tumble out. That happened the other day when a friend asked about Bruce Weigl and thought maybe he should start writing about other things and leave the war behind him, that perhaps focusing so much on Vietnam was limiting in some way, and I began to think about a number of writers who have focused closely and not repetitively, but often on that "splendid little war" that so many of us share in some way. I wondered how they could possibly stop writing about it, not why they should continue to do so.

When I walk through the hill country here in Texas, or hike into the Organ Mountains outside of Las Cruces, or stroll down a trail in the Big Thicket, paddle a canoe through the bays of the Texas coast or down the Guadalupe River when there is no drought, I feel more alive than I do at almost any other time, even when, no, especially when, I am alone.

But when I see these things, find myself away from other people, way out on the still waters of Espiritu Santo Bay or between lines of hills where I cannot hear cars on the highway or on a path hiking up to Dripping Springs outside Las Cruces, I find myself not exactly flashing back, with all the unpleasant connotations that accompany that phrase, but seeing once again the hills and low mountains of the Central Highlands in Vietnam, hearing the waters of the South China Sea at Chu Lai, looking again into a schoolyard in Pleiku and seeing a giant Buddha smashed apart.

The other day, I had to replace two tires on my Ranger and went to NTB, a subsidiary of Sears. The salesman's name was Jesse something and, as he looked out at the rains beating down on the parking lot, he said that whenever it rained it reminded him of the monsoons in Vietnam. I told him I had been there in 1967-68 and he said, "No shit, man. Me, too. I was with the first of the 46th, Americal Division. I laughed and told him I'd gone over on the *USNS Gordon* with the 198th Light Infantry Brigade. He'd been on the same ship. We talked about it for a while, all the time looking out at the rain. He's not a writer and he doesn't suffer from a bad case of PTSD, but his war is always with him, too.

I do not know how anyone who was there, whether in combat or not, could avoid those moments or why they would ever want to do so. Another friend was talking about Christmas in Vietnam the other night and that day for me remains hazier than most days. I didn't get drunk often when I was stationed in Pleiku, but I did on December 25, 1967. Just something about the holidays.

I had bought a fifth of Ruffino's Chianti, the only portable drink other than beer the Club had on that day, and wandered down to the berm. The 555th Engineers had bulldozed the thing and the bunker line was right in front of it and down the hill before you got to the Air Force Base and the city lay a scrub thicket and, if I remember correctly, a small village walled in with bamboo. I sat on top of the berm looking down at the lights of the AFB and the comparative darkness of Pleiku and drank until I drained the bottle.

The truce had held fairly well that Christmas, probably in preparation for the truce that would mark the Tet Offensive of 1968, only a little more than a month away, but occasionally, I saw a flare go off and heard what had to be some artillery unit blasting away just to make noise to celebrate Christmas. After I finished the bottle, I lay back on the red dirt of the berm, saw the same stars I can still see here in Texas and fell asleep.

Not a big story. Nothing happened. No one dropped any mortars in the compound. No one that I know of got hurt. When I woke up in the morning, I had a hangover, but no one got angry at my not being where I was supposed to be in "the appropriate uniform at the appropriate time" that morning after Christmas. It's a hell of a moment to have memories about — a drunken night when absolutely nothing out of the ordinary happened.

But it's part of the reason, not just the anger, not just the violence and death, that I think writers like Weigl and Ehrhart and Komunyakaa and so many others can't not write about Vietnam or, at least, must come back to it frequently. It's always there, sitting in the landscapes of our minds, even for those of us who didn't wander into danger very often.

Driving Somewhere

As I drive south from Fargo, North Dakota, determined to make Council Bluffs before going to sleep, the radio forecasts snow in northern Iowa with temperatures dropping to 18 during the night. It is 9 o'clock and I am entering a peculiar zone in my driving, my mind in two pieces, one focusing on the road, the other flashing back to other long drives I have made in the past. In this state, I pay attention to the highway, reacting as needed, but I can really see nothing, no spot on the route will come back to my memory, but it is dark and I drove through this area only five days ago. I stop momentarily and take a caffeine hit through Diet Coke. I am smoking again, but will stop when I am back in Texas.

I drive through Sioux City and the weather reports are letting up. There will be no snow here tomorrow. I am tempted to stop, but on long drives I have this feeling that I must make my goals or something, I do not know what, will happen. As I leave Sioux City behind, I am driving 80 miles an hour, coasting, and am passed by a semi pulling two trailers. I smile as I read the sign on the side: Batesville Casket Company and think of Janet Leigh in her shower at the Bates Motel.

But I begin to relive a drive I took 23 years ago, nonstop from Austin, Texas, to Washington, D.C. I was engaged to Linda and with the passing days and weeks had become more and more convinced that I had made a mistake, that I simply did not want to be married, not to anyone, not at this stage in my life. Austin had been nirvana for me in the few short months I had lived there. When Don and Allen and I were discharged from the Army back in December, we drove straight through, taking turns at the wheel and at sleeping. The first two nights in Austin we spent with Ann and her two room mates. For a couple of years the three of us would share a house near the University, and in those first months had a great time repainting the interior in black with day-glo highlights. As I said, a long time ago.

That day I realized I didn't want to marry Linda, I agonized over how to tell her and was tempted to just call and break it off. But that seemed too easy, much too easy, for me after a relationship that had lasted two years, had seen us marching together against the war in the streets of Washington, making love almost every night, taking her twins out to the parks on the weekends, getting high together on life instead of on various chemical substances. Linda deserved better than a brief phone call and that time in my life deserved something more monumental to mark its passing. So, I decided to return to Washington.

At 9 a.m. the next morning, I threw some clothes into a bag and filled my cooler with beer and cokes, left a note for Don and Allen and headed northeast from Austin to Washington in my 1966 VW convertible. The trip took 27 hours one-way, non-stop except for fueling the car every 250 miles or so. The first eight or nine hours were all in Texas: Austin to Dallas on I-35, Dallas to Texarkana on I-30. One problem with living in the heart of Texas is that you have to drive so far to really feel you've made progress. When I lived in Washington, I could drive through four states in the same time it took me to reach the Arkansas border. But the highways were good and the miles rolled under me.

Late that night, 2 or 3 a.m., I drove along the Blue Ridge in Virginia and a million fireflies made the Shenandoah Valley glow out the driver's side window. The Milky Way was above and below me as I took steep turns, barely awake, zoning out as I am zoned out driving through Iowa. But this time, I began to fall asleep, and my car drifted out of my lane towards the cliffs on the left side of the road. I suspect I would be dead now except for a truck driver who raced up on my tail and blinked his lights, blowing his air horn loudly, jolting me back to life. I was able to swing the car back into my lane, then stopped and got out, just standing there, almost drunk from exhaustion, watched the fireflies below me, winking in and out, and sat down under a tree for what seemed like hours.

I drove on down the highway and stopped at the first diner I came to. This was the first real stop I had made and at the diner I drank cup after cup of coffee and I do not normally drink coffee, got strung out, tense, jittery, and headed back east and north, anxious to have the trip over, the trip almost becoming the meaning, the form pushing the substance of the trip, my split with Linda, back into the recesses of my mind. As I drove on, I began to see things along the road that were not really there, bushes became animals leaping onto the road in front of me, the shadows were alive, and slowly, slowly, the fireflies began to disappear.

As the sun rose that morning, I continued to fight sleep, continued to make the VW move as quickly as possible, the drive becoming the thing itself, punishment for what I was going to do, pushing guilt back and back. I irrationally began to get mad at Linda, blamed her for the whole thing, for my near accident on the Blue Ridge Skyline, for my driving to Washington, though I knew she was not to blame.

I took the beltway around Washington, exited at one of the Silver Spring exits, and pulled the VW into her parking space. It was 2 p.m. and Linda was still at work. I opened her door with my key and walked into the apartment, so familiar, like I still belonged there. I walked back to our bedroom, took my clothes off and fell asleep almost instantly.

Not until 9 that evening did Linda wake me up. She climbed into bed and kissed me awake, her body pressed against mine. We made love that night, my body settling into familiar rhythms, hers knowing mine instantly. Even in doing it, I knew that I should not, but I was still on the highway, still in that zone where you do things without really thinking. A sad comment, I know, but truthful.

The whole thing would have been much easier if she had gotten mad at me, had kicked me out of her house when I told her after we got up, after we went into the kitchen and had a beer, that I did not want to get married, that no, there was no one else, and there was not, that I simply was not ready for marriage, but she didn't. She was the very soul of reason, very controlled, very cool. She didn't cry, didn't scream at me, didn't try to get me to change my mind. When I told her I needed to leave right away, to get back to Austin for classes, she told me to spend the night, to rest. The next morning, she made breakfast for me after the kids had gone to school. And then she kissed me goodbye.

I'm glad I made the trip. It would not have been right to end things with a simple phone call. But I wish, somehow, she had been nasty. But if she had, it would have been just for me. I hope now that when I left she closed the door and laughed, howled, shook with joy that she had gotten out of a situation that she did not want. But I don't really believe that.

Just out of Washington, I picked up two hitchhikers headed for Memphis, Tennessee, and we smoked their grass and talked. When I got tired, I turned the driving over to them and slept until we got to their place. I drove back to Austin.

As I pull into the Council Bluffs Holiday Inn, my thoughts are filled with Linda, with that trip to Washington almost 25 years ago. And tomorrow, tomorrow, when I drive through Missouri and Kansas and Oklahoma and more than halfway through Texas, I will enter that zone again, my driving will be safe, but automatic. And I will be back in the past, always in the past, probably in the sixties, my signifying decade. I will be driving to Key West just after being drafted, with Anthony in the car, or maybe to Arizona to be with my sister when she had some problems or perhaps on a long trip to Manhattan in 1964, just after graduating from college, to work in the World's Fair, but really, just to be alive in New York.

I carry my luggage into the hotel, fill out the registration form, and go to bed. Alone, but not really. I am never more in company than I am when I get in my car and head across country.

Studying Foreign Languages In Graduate School

My second semester in graduate school, after the English Department at UT told me that being able to read and speak Vietnamese would not count toward satisfying the graduate school's language requirements, I dove head first into German, taking a 15 semester hour total-immersion program in twelve weeks. During those weeks, I lived, thought and "dated" in German. I recommend that kind of program for anyone who is serious about languages.

The woman of my German summer was an international student from Grenoble named Petra. Her mother was German and her father French, but they had signed their own separate peace during the second of the world wars. Petra had light, wispy blonde hair and was close to 5' 10" tall, slender, but not skinny. We lived together only for that one summer and spoke what must have been incredibly bad German during the entire relationship.

One of the things I liked about Petra was her mixed background. Perhaps because her father was French, she harbored no real resentment of Viet-Nam veterans. After all, the second Indochina War was really an extension of the first, which had ended at Dien Bien Phu with the defeat of the French. And, because her mother was German, she did not feel she could be overly critical of anyone involved even in a less than just war.

I do not want to give a false impression. I did not experience much overt hostility in graduate school because I had been in Vietnam, most people simply did not care. From time to time, though, some of the faculty members exhibited incredible moments of smug superiority that I, more often than not, simply laughed at. That summer, only a few days before I met Petra, I had gone with my friend Laura to a party being given for a history professor who had been denied tenure though he had been named the teacher of the year in the School of Humanities and Social Sciences by the students. The party was a "pariahs" party and one of the leading campus anti-war faculty members spent almost half an hour bemoaning the fact that he had been unable to demonstrate his pacifist fervor by going to jail because he had been found to be 4-F during a pre-induction physical.

When he looked at me, his heart murmuring pacifically, and smirked after saying that, I merely told him that a few of us had been given the opportunity to risk something for peace by standing up, even after we had been to Vietnam, and saying aloud, under circumstances that could hurt our futures, that we felt our government was wrong and that too many people had already been killed.

But this is about Petra and a wonderful summer, not about politics or the war. I met Petra on the first day of that German class and we hit it off beautifully. I knew a little French and she spoke English almost fluently, but during the six hours of class each day, we could only speak German and, to reinforce the immersion, Petra and I agreed to talk with each other only in that language outside of class. Part of the attraction, I suppose, was the fact that we were both older than the other students, all undergraduates trying to get their language requirement out of the way quickly. Petra was 29 that summer and had just completed her doctoral dissertation in classics. I was, at 27, just beginning my doctorate in English.

That first night, we went to a movie showing at the Commons on campus, a film called *Die Brucke* (the Bridge), in German with English subtitles. If you have not seen the film, I recommend it highly as one of the great anti-war films of the period. Its subject is a German school for boys during the late stages of World War II and you see the boys develop as young and passionate warriors for the Third Reich. It reminded me of Golding's *Lord of the Flies* only with a firm sense of brown-shirted discipline. In an awesome scene, the American army attacks the area where the school is located and the boys decide to defend the fatherland. The good-natured, fumbling Americans assume the boys are only children and try to befriend them. In the only English in the film, one of the children shoots an American and we hear him scream "You bastards!" as he dies.

It is difficult to carry on a discussion about a film when your native language is English and your partner's language is French and you are conversing in yet a third language that you have both only begun to learn that same day. Aside from *guten abend, gesundheit* and *auf wiedersehen*, our German was limited to asking each other what our names were and how we were feeling. Because we had dictionaries and the desire to communicate verbally, we learned to say *Ich liebe dich* that same night when we went to bed together for the first time.

Neither of us had the language for love-making in German. But we learned the vocabulary and conjugations over the next few weeks with special cram sessions every evening. There is no better language lab in the world than sitting in bed and touching and playing "name the parts," then laughing and starting over. Such a catalogue might make an interesting poem, but I was not interested in writing poetry in those days. In German she would ask, "How do you say what I am doing now?" as she would run her hand lightly over my chest. And I would try to tell her, in German.

In bed, under oak trees on campus, by Lake Travis, wherever we were, we would read Hölderlin to each other and Peter Weiss and Schiller and Peter Handke and Rilke and so many others, all in the original German. We were not fluent, not even terribly good with the language, but, as the weeks passed, we could understand enough and knew enough to speak the words and sentences with the correct emphasis and rhythm. We acted out *Ein Andere Kommt nach Deutchsland* (A Stranger Comes to Germany) and marveled at its simplicity of language. We took turns shouting Peter Handke's *Publikumsbeschimpfung* (Offending an Audience) and fell laughing into bed. We listened to tapes of Marlene Deitrich and of Lotte Lenya singing Kurt Weill songs and saw still more German films. We never, in the twelve weeks we were together, said a single word in English or in French to each other.

When the class was over and Petra graduated, I was her only guest and took her to the airport immediately afterwards. After she flew back to France, we wrote a few times, always in German, and then the letters faded away.

I remember Petra perfectly after more than two decades, the sound of her voice whispering "*ich liebe dich*," the way she looked when she dove naked into the water at Hippie Hollow, the arch of her back when she dried her hair after a swim, the way her bare feet felt next to mine, the sheer wonder of her pale hair as the dry wind blew it into my face while she napped, the slightly salty taste of her skin in the hot Texas summer sun. She will always remain as she was then and I would not know her now in her late fifties. As poorly versed as we were in that language that is not considered a language of love, but of war, German will always be for me an erotic language.

I can no longer speak German and can read it, once again, only with the help of a dictionary, but when I want to read a Rilke poem, I enjoy reading it aloud as he wrote it and then reading a good translation. Sometimes, when I read a poem by Hölderlin, I hear it in her voice. I suspect Petra kept up with her German, at least more so than I did. She would have greater need for it in Grenoble than I have had in San Antonio. Perhaps, though, she lives in Paris now or Berlin. Wherever she is, she will always be in Austin at age 29, walking down the street or talking to me in husky German, or she will be asleep on our bed, breathing softly in those early morning hours before we awaken and walk together to campus.

Getting Married

I buy a suit. I am aware that every day men or women buy suits, but I have never bought a suit. It is a beige suit, nondescript. The suit can be worn for all important functions. I pack the suit in a suit bag and I put the suit bag in a closet. The suit suits me, not just for a marriage but because of job hunts to come.

It will be a simple wedding. Susan makes banners that are Christian, but, thank the gods, are not saccharine. We find a priest in Texas who does not care that I am not Catholic, that I have been to no church in twenty years. While the priest does not care if I am Christian or not, he does care that we have not been to pre-Canna conference or to summer camp for soon-to-be-marrieds. The priest is best friends with one of Susan's roommates. When she asks, he fills out all the paper work for us to be married in St. Louis, at the Newman Center of St. Louis University.

I go to conference for five consecutive nights. At conference, I am told that men are like light bulbs and women are like irons. The priest is talking about sex. The priest is saying that with a flick of an erotic switch the man turns on, but women take a while to reach appropriate heat for ironing out wrinkles. When Susan and I get home that night, I turn on the lights and she has an insatiable desire to press my clothes. We are advised, too, to purchase a duplex and let others pay for our house by renting for exorbitant rates.

Susan is in St. Louis fighting her mother, insisting upon a simple wedding. The Newman Center is set, a priest has been briefed on what will happen. My best man, Don, climbs on his Triumph bike in West Lafayette, Indiana, and heads west to Missouri. I get in my Ford Pinto, now a solid member of the middle class, and drive north as far as Waco before I realize that my suit is in a bag in the closet. I return to San Antonio, get my new suit, and then drive straight through to St. Louis. I do not notice anything along the highway. I am zoned out. I drink four beers just crossing Texas where it was still perfectly legal to drink and drive.

Don and I stay with a cousin of mine in Clayton, Missouri. We go to the wedding rehearsal fortified with beer and watch Susan's sisters carry in the banners, listen to a pretty good folk trio sing Paul

Stookey's "Wedding Song" and three other trendy folk tunes about getting married. My mother has arrived and is hosting a rehearsal dinner at a nice restaurant. Tonight, I will see Susan for the last time until the wedding. I tell Don about light bulbs and irons and we drink and laugh. The dinner comes off okay.

I do not remember much about the next night except that I am uptight and am drinking too much and smoking. I have not seen Susan for more than two hours since I arrived in St. Louis. The day of the wedding, I put on my new suit, a frilly white shirt and black bow tie. My hands are shaking and Don has to tie the tie. He hugs me. "Hey, man, it's good, cool." I consider asking Don to let me take his bike while he drives my Pinto, but decide not to.

When I walk into the chapel, I hear the trio, all acoustic guitars, tuning up. Don and I get ready to do the "down the aisle" thing. I am sure everyone must think Susan is pregnant, but she is not. This is an act of volition. It has been years since anyone pointed a gun at me. We will not have our only child for five more years.

I am numb as I walk from the waiting room to the front of the chapel. Don manages to keep me on the right track. The priest we had asked to make it official waits for us and beside him is a tall man in flaming red robes. He is not part of the script for this production. He is a bishop, a friend of Susan's grandmother. He has decided to concelebrate the mass. I look around and see the banners Susan had sewn hanging behind the altar, see the trio, hear them break into a folksy version of the "Wedding March," hear rustling as the crowd stands up, look down the long aisle to the back of the chapel. Susan's sisters walk down the aisle. Then, dressed in white, veil over her face, her long hair up, a single pearl descending on gold lace to her bodice, Susan walks toward me. I almost panic.

Surrounded by institutions, both physical and emotional, that I have resisted since I was fifteen years old, my knees grow weak and I almost bolt out of the room. But Don holds my arm and Susan holds the rest of me with just her appearance, a faint smile. Her brother walks with her, her hand on his arm. I cannot hear the music. I cannot see the room full of people. It is all white and golden and I am lost and I am happy to be lost.

FLASHFORWARD: 1983. I am running the library at a small Catholic university though I am not Catholic. My son Stephen is five years old. For various reasons, none of which have to do with my job, I join the Church. The reasons are complex and are not really a part of this story. Aside from marrying Susan, I hadn't been inside a church since I was fifteen. When I publish my first book of poems I dedicate it to my son with the hope that his generation will not have to face its own Vietnam.

The ceremony has become more complex with the arrival of the bishop. Don is astonished when the man in red walks up to read and instructs him. "Kneel in front of me," he whispers, "and hold the Bible up, open in your hands, above your head, so I can read." Later, Don says, "I thought he was shitting me!" He kneels and the bishop reads, admonishes us in many Catholic ways about bringing up children in the Church, about Susan's being a good wife, about my being a good provider, all the stuff we had carefully deleted from the ceremony. The rest of it goes like we planned. I speak the vows I have written and Susan says hers to me. We have them still somewhere, stashed away. The ceremony ends and we race out of the church.

For a long moment, I stand and look at the Triumph. Damn, I think. Why can't we just hop on and ride off? I hold Susan for a moment. We kiss.

Places to Grow

I first drove down U.S. 281 to Corpus Christi and turned right on US 77 more than twenty years ago. I had been married for two years and Susan and I were taking a summer break from graduate school to lie in the sun and swim in the warm waters of the Gulf of Mexico. The landscape was ragged, raw, no mountains to thrill the soul, no thicket to cast shade over the hot two-lane blacktop highway. Corn and cotton grew within two feet of the highway and every once in a while an old service station, one with those yellowish glass balls that showed the fuel, would appear, needing paint, peeling in the salty air blowing in from Corpus Christi Bay or Laguna Madre a few miles east.

At that time of the year, a traveler could see migrant workers in the fields, picking various kinds of crops for piece wages. Hard stoop labor, so hot and sweaty, so low-paying that most American citizens would not consider the work. Today, as we grumble about the increasing numbers of undocumented aliens coming into the country, we don't always remember that they are taking jobs our children, our cousins, brothers and sisters would not consider doing even for the kinds of wages being paid today.

Something about that stretch of highway has always spoken to me, telling me stories about the people who lived there, not just the migrant workers, but also the owners, the middle-class, the people who scrabbled their livings from that barren stretch of land. When I started working at St. Mary's University in San Antonio, many of the children of those workers and owners were among my students. Not a stretch of land anyone could easily call sacred or spiritual, but that hard, sweaty place provides a living for some who could not find jobs and housing elsewhere, people who have little or no education, people without even a green card to help them find easier employment. Many live there their entire lives and watch their children grow and go to school and, in many cases, on to the university where I work. Their grandchildren occasionally enroll and become doctors and lawyers, businessmen, officers in the Air Force and Army.

Since leaving Vietnam and getting out of the Army to march against that war, I had been almost single-mindedly opposed to war and to militarism, proud to have rejected Officer Candidate School and an offer to put me up for a direct commission back in the late 60s. When people asked me why, I always said that in a country made up of aristocrats and workers, only the working class can live honorably. That was an honest sentiment, though young and naive. What a shock it was to begin work in San Antonio, military city of Texas, and see so many of my brighter students graduate in uniform with commissions and march off stage to the military with their families screaming and shouting. Many of them had come to my little private university on R.O.T.C. scholarships and were the first people in their families ever to go to college, much less graduate into something other than the laboring classes. They were proud of their accomplishments and I was proud of them.

Generational evolution came out of the muggy soup of South Texas, from the fields along the sides of US 77, and as we drove, no air conditioning, no steep division from the land that you find along the interstates, I could not help but think that for years, in its own, raw and life-sucking way, this place has given nourishment.

But, as I had learned playing in the woods across from a housing project and thinking by a small lake in the middle of a war, sometimes what seems spiritually satisfying to us changes because of personal experience, because of things extraneous to the land, because of what we do or what people we care about do. Then the same heat and salty wetness is transformed. No longer spiritual, it becomes hell, not because of what it is, not because it has changed dramatically, but because of what we carry with us.

That happened for me along US 77 a few years ago. My son, who was in his junior year in high school left home without permission to join the thousands of high school and college students celebrating the rites of spring on South Padre Island. He called the next afternoon, to apologize for running off and to tell me he and his best friend were headed home. "I'm sorry, Dad," he said, "I really screwed up." He did not know exactly how badly he had screwed up, though. Two hours later, we got a call from Kingsville, Texas. He and his friend had been arrested for possession of a controlled substance, a second degree felony. Since my son's seventeenth birthday had happened in February, he would be treated as an adult.

This isn't really about my son. It's about the place, a place I had admired and had not ever really been a part of. That year, from March until July, I drove those same highways every single Wednesday so my son could report for Pretrial Supervision and I was appalled at the sterility I saw. The old service stations are gone, replaced by shiny new automated stations where you don't really even need to see anyone, just run your gasoline credit card through a magnetic strip reader, or they have allied themselves with fast food chains: Mobil Oil/Arby's, Texaco/ McDonald's, Exxon/Subway. The highway is patrolled regularly by the border patrol, "la Migra," and huge machines harvest the cotton and barley. What remains is the heat and the hot, muggy, salty air. But the place hasn't changed significantly. I know the people still work hard, still send their children on to school and college, but for me the spiritual quality has largely vanished and may never return.

I live in a north-side suburb of San Antonio, Texas. Middle-class, well-educated people live here. It is an incredible distance from the projects I once called home. My next door neighbor on the right is a sports reporter for the local newspaper and has the top-rated sports show on local television. On the other side of my house, my neighbor is an engineer working for an aircraft company. Within five blocks six different university professors have built their homes.

As so many suburbanites have, I have found a real sense of satisfaction in my own backyard. When I dug a pond five years ago and strained my back with the labor, I began to appreciate the work other people who have chopped through the caliche have experienced. I suspect that my pond and my back yard mean much more to me than they would have if I had hired someone else to do the work. Since March, I have spent hours each day sitting in the yard, writing and reading, looking at the pond. I have seen water lilies bloom and the pale yellow of Louisiana Iris shooting up out of the water. This week, with my son safely off in college, some months after my last drive down U.S. 77, I have begun digging again—a second pond that will be a few feet north of the first and overlap it. A small waterfall will trickle from the new pond to the old and the sound of water will be added to the other sounds in the suburban wilderness that is my home.

I have come to think that we have to earn the right to have a place we can call our own, a place that can have lasting meaning for us. Living in an urban community that sneers at the very word "suburb," I confess to loving my home and not because of the house and yard that were here when we moved in with our six year old son, but because of what we have made of it with our own hands. The fish in my pond, the tropical night-blooming Juno lily, the pale yellow Sulfurea and the Queen of Whites, the cattails and parrotsfeather, purple pickerel, water poppies and water lettuce, all of these things grow here because of my own labor and that work has made me a part of the place.

When we came back from Kingsville, after the trial, we sat in the backyard facing the pond until it grew dark and talked of what had happened. Healing began that night.

What happened to my son along a road I had once romanticized convinces me, almost, that places cannot, by themselves be imbued with spirit, that that sense of the sacred is something that grows inside us and must be earned, not merely acquired through resting in a place for a day or two, for a week, for years.

Thoreau went to the woods to confront life, to drive it into a corner, to examine it. But life does not always allow itself not to be examined and we do not have to go to the woods. It happens every time we open our eyes. And the place that calls us might be found a continent away or years in the past, or in the inner city, or in our own backyards, even if we live in suburbia. But there is a problem with such places. They can and do change in a heartbeat.

Coming to Terms with Dad

From the eastern side of a tall sand dune a few hundred yards back from the beach line on Matagorda Island, I can see for miles out into the Gulf of Mexico. Although I am almost alone on the island, only a few people on duty at the USFWS Station near the ferry landing, the Gulf is not a lonely place and I can see shrimpers working fairly close to shore and, as the sun rises behind me, the fading lights of the off-shore oil rigs blinking on and off even farther out. I am wearing open sandals and the sand blowing against my ankles adds to the side of the dune that stretches twenty feet above me or blows up and over the sea oats that lean back toward the mainland and away from the stiff breezes at the crest to begin forming secondary dunes. On the western side of the dune trail goat-foot morning glories and gulf crotons stretch out, planting roots in patterns that help keep the sand stable.

I do not know why I hauled the 17 and ½ foot Mohawk canoe, dusty from lack of use this summer, onto the top of the Cherokee before daylight and packed a cooler for what would be a long hot day, stowed my fishing net, rod and reel, and fish bucket, and drove two hours down US-181. My wife asked me that the day before and I could not give a very good answer.

Perhaps the only reason is linkage and in a place that is not profuse with vegetation except in its inner swales, a tying together with a part of my life that I have not visited in more than thirty years. When I was very young, my family and I visited my grandmother in a wilderness area along the northern Gulf Coast of Florida each summer. I was fascinated by a small island our family had, for generations, called "Patty's Island" out in the middle of Wakulla Bay. Equidistant between two creeks that emptied into that small body of salt water, the island was little more than a spit of sand separating the small bay from the much larger Appalachee Bay.

One day, my father had taken me fishing, way out past the island into deeper waters and a sudden storm blew up, dark gray clouds, repeated jagged bolts of lightning, wind that whipped the normally smooth surface of Appalachee Bay into large swells. The outboard motor on the small boat wouldn't start and we drifted in towards land several miles from my grandmother's house.

I was not frightened. "Don't worry," my father said. "We don't have to do a damned thing except ride it out. If we need to, we can put ashore on Patty's Island." I remember enjoying the storm, being out on the water, tossing up and down in that little twelve-foot boat, yelling and laughing. The whole time we drifted, rain stinging my bare back and chest, he disassembled the motor, greased all the parts, and put it back together. When he pulled on the rope, the engine coughed back to life and he told me to take us back home.

Patty's Island is much like the barrier islands on the Texas coast, only so small that no one can build on it. I have walked across it a few times, perhaps fifty yards, and stood on a very tiny sand beach that faces the larger bay and waded carefully through the brackish water on the mainland side. Like Matagorda Island, it is covered with sea oats and morning glories, is occupied by fiddler crabs and sand fleas and horseshoe crabs when the moon is full. It is only a half mile or so from shore and I have swum the distance a few times.

I have come to Matagorda Island, I suppose, to remember, to build links between the me that is approaching 54 years old and the me at nine years old, the small boy who took the handle of the outboard motor and steered in between Patty's Island and the East Goose Creek oyster bars to bring a small boat through driving rain and beach it on the sand of the tidal flats at Wakulla Beach. I am not a naturalist, not as good an environmentalist as I ought to be, but barrier islands have fascinated me since those days that Patty's Island stood off the coast of Florida and I looked at it, wanting to visit, when I was very young.

So this morning I have driven to a different coast with a different kind of vessel riding on top of the Jeep. I would not have an old 5 horsepower outboard motor, only my paddles, and my father has been dead for more than 35 years. Maybe that's why I came to the beach—to say hello again and goodbye.

Today, though, while thinking about my past and about my father, I am worrying about the weather. The wind is picking up and I do not think I will be able to put my canoe into Espiritu Santo Bay and paddle the four miles out to the island. I can drift back, the wind always blows to shore along the Gulf Coast of Texas, midway through the Coastal Bend, but fighting strong headwinds in a small canoe is rarely worth the effort. What I want to do is get the canoe in the water and paddle out before the heat builds and the wind picks up.

I stopped first at the Coast Guard Station at Port O'Connor and looked out at Espiritu Santo Bay. You cannot see Matagorda Island because of an intervening island made when the IntraCoastal Canal was cut through the bays. Barges move from Florida through Texas on that canal and, along the way, pass the habitat of the Whooping Cranes at the Aransas Wildlife Refuge across Espiritu Santo from Matagorda Island.

The winds are mild, after all, and not many boats are on the bay. I am able to paddle away from shore without too much worry about being run over by power boats and shrimpers, a constant problem for people who put out from shore in quiet transports, without motors, without sails. No thick layer of clouds covers the sky, only the normal bank of cumulus clouds out over the Gulf and, by 9 a.m., it has grown hot and I am sticky with the salty air by the time I have paddled two miles across the bay and approach the tidal flats of Matagorda Island. Moving slowly along the western shore of the barrier island, the lee side, I can hear, only a mile to the west across the narrow sandy island, the Gulf of Mexico send waves crashing onto the beaches, waves that would easily flip my canoe.

The water in the bay is shallow, only about two to five feet deep for miles and miles, but occasionally broken into deeper channels. I stop paddling and drift over sea weeds, letting what wind there is push the canoe to the north, away from shore a little, but tracking the coast. After a few minutes, I tie the ends of the net, the bottom lined with small weights, to the last strut at the stern of the canoe and feel the whole thing shudder to a stop as I throw the net behind me. The canoe lurches as if I had dropped a heavy sea anchor overboard to drag it along the bottom.

If I were a shrimper, I would rev up the two diesel engines in my boat and try to make two to three knots in the bay waters. Behind me, my net would stretch 78 feet back with two wooden "doors" keeping the front open, and, flying above the scoop, dozens of sea gulls and other water birds would dive down to capture the small fish and shrimp that escape through the opening, frequently wounded, unable to swim easily. The gulls would wait as I culled the trash fish, fingerling speckled trout and red fish, jelly fish, sting rays, all but the shrimp, from the net and threw it overboard. Then they would shriek and dive into the water.

I am thinking about the shrimpers, I suppose, because my father had always wanted that life, the life of a professional shrimper, but it is not a life that appeals to me. I have met shrimpers, have been out as a volunteer deckhand on a shrimp boat that lumbered along the beaches of the Gulf of Mexico, sometimes ten or twelve miles out into the Gulf, and it is hot, sweaty, debilitating work. The men and, now, women who trawl for shrimp in Gulf waters have a difficult life, practicing a business with low profits and one that is absolutely dependant, as is the life of a farmer, on the whims of nature and upon man's apparent desire to ruin the environment that provides the crop. Shrimpers, though, are like so many of the rest of us: when they finish a beer they heave it over the side with the rest of their trash and help foul the waters even more.

But I am not a shrimper and I am not in a shrimp boat. The canoe moves erratically, if at all, as I paddle again and manage to drag the very small net forward about ten feet before throwing the paddle down and pulling the net back into the canoe. The net is a muddy mess, coated with seaweed, its basket brimming with the same kind of trash the shrimpers haul in. I separate a dozen or so white shrimp (*penaeus setiferus*) and a half dozen brown shrimp (*penaeus aztecas*) and put them quickly into the bucket that I had earlier filled with seawater and drape the net over the prow of the canoe to dry.

The white shrimp I will have for lunch later, boiled over an open fire on the island if I can find enough driftwood to make a fire; the brown shrimp are for bait. The drought in South Texas has affected the shrimp breeding grounds of Espiritu Santo Bay and the other bays that depend on fresh water runoff from the rivers to reduce salinity. The shrimp I catch are much smaller than the shrimp I would have caught only a few years ago. It is a delicate balance, this balance between the rivers, the bays and the ocean. The largest shrimp swim in the Gulf of Mexico, and breed there, but the bays and estuaries are the hatcheries and the shrimp that hatch there live in the bays until they are large and ready to breed. Then they swim through the openings in the islands to get to deeper water.

When I have the better shrimp culled, enough to eat enough to use for bait, I paddle the canoe to shore and take a quick swim to get the slime from the net off my hands and arms and to let the net dry in the hot sun before folding it and heading back out into the bay.

High tide today is at 11 a.m. and I am back on the bay as the water begins to race out through the cuts in Pass Cavallo or around the southwest end of the island at Cedar Bayou. It's a hot, lazy day and I let the eight pound test line drift out behind me as the canoe moves on its own across the weedy bottom of the bay.

What I hope to catch today are two or three speckled trout, enough for dinner before I load the canoe back onto the Cherokee and drive back home. Huck Finn says, just before being joined by the Duke and the King and being forced back into civilization, that "it's lovely being on a raft"; it is equally lovely lying down in a canoe and drifting, a line strung out behind you, baited with a live shrimp, not paying attention to much of anything, just drifting and thinking, falling half asleep.

The last time I came here, I had taken the ferry from Port O'Connor. It is restricted to pedestrians only. The only motorized traffic on the island is used by the U.S. Park and Wildlife Service. I walked through the state park and along old roads that take me to the Matagorda Lighthouse and across the eroding runways placed there in the 1940s as the nation got ready for the second of the great wars and used the island for bombing practice. Matagorda Island is not a "pure" wilderness area. The scars that we put on it in the past will remain for years to come, probably even surviving a storm surge from all but the most powerful hurricane.

As I drift in the bay, I am also thinking a little bit about the skipper of the *Hai Ba Trung*, a Vietnamese shrimper I met when I had breakfast this morning. His job is the work my father would have preferred. When shrimpers gather, they talk about shrimp and shrimping, just as the rest of us talk about our own work when we get together. Here at Port O'Connor, the shrimpers complain much as the farmers north of here complain, about the drought, about the need for long, soaking rains, perhaps even a wish for one of the tropical storms now brewing on the east coast of South America and heading for landfall in Central America to make the cut past Yucatan and enter the Gulf, blowing westerly, miles out from Galveston Island and then turning north across Matagorda Island and Espiritu Santo Bay and on up to San Antonio and the Hill Country to wash back down through flooding rivers until the water sucked up from the oceans pours back down into the bays to bolster the next crop of shrimp.

In the 1970s, the average shrimp boat caught 600-700 pounds of shrimp each day, by the late 1980s that average catch had dropped to 400-500 pounds per day. In the 1990s, though there are fewer shrimpers, the per boat catch has dropped even more. The shrimpers blame the weather more than anything else, this current cycle of drought, though there is a healthy share of blame dumped upon foreign, meaning Mexican, shrimpers fishing in U.S. coastal waters and there remains an uneasy state of peaceful coexistence between the Vietnamese and "American" shrimpers. That state of grudging truce is far preferable to the armed warfare of the late 70s and early 80s when several Vietnamese boats were shot at and burned.

I think my father's dream might have been good for him. He wanted to live the kind of life these men and women are living. He was brought up on coastal waters and fished almost every summer day of his life while he was a young boy. Each year of his life was, somehow, measured by the sea: WWII in the Merchant Marine, pleasure fishing even when he was at home in Florida and in Texas, and afterwards as a member of the Masters, Mates and Pilots Union, until that life ended when his ship vanished at sea. His dream was natural, the dream of an entrepreneur who knows his field and wants independence from the bosses. Still, it would have been a hard life.

I am awakened when a sharp strike moves the rod in my hand and, for a few minutes play the game of death with what turns out to be a twelve-inch speckled trout, much too small to keep. Over the next half hour, I pull in six more, letting all of them off the hook without taking them out of the water. I have caught enough— enough fish, enough shrimp, enough sun— though I have caught no fish to keep. It's three o'clock and I paddle back to shore, pushed by the now strong wind from the Gulf and then pull the canoe for awhile, walking along the edge of the shore to get the kinks out of my shoulders and back and because I do not want to fight the wind with paddles. By five o'clock I am back where I had parked the Cherokee.

I start a small fire on the beach and boil the remaining white shrimp in fresh water with a shrimp broil mix of spices before throwing them into a small baggie and placing them in the cooler. I let them grow cold as I pull the canoe out of the water and tie it down again on top of the Cherokee and stow the other gear in the back.

It has been a long day and there are still two more hours of daylight. I sit down in shallow salt water and eat the cold shrimp and drink a Lone Star beer. I watch a small shrimp boat out in the bay, trundling through the water, and drink to the captain and the deckhands. I do not think there will be many shrimpers left at the end of the next decade. They are harvesters of the sea, they do not plant their crop, and their sons and daughters are not following them in their profession. From a distance, watching the boat plow through the water, almost seeming not to move, dozens of sea gulls following behind, I can almost buy into the captain's dream. But it is only the long day, the feeling of contentment in eating the shrimp I have caught, drinking an ice cold beer. These are boatman's dreams and dreams almost reinforced by the cries of water birds. They are not for me.

A True Story about an Old Woman and Poetry

1.

I had been teaching a small workshop at a medical center. Eight rather small, one-floor buildings surround a large pond filled with water lilies and a stone fountain. The buildings were all labeled: Counseling Center, Substance Abuse Center, Hospice, Special School, Chapel, Cafeteria, Reconciliation Center, Administration. The grounds were always bright green, well-manicured, with pecan, ash and live oak trees. I enjoyed walking through the area on breaks from class and sitting near the pond for a few minutes each evening after teaching.

I first saw her on a Monday evening. She sat on one of the wooden benches positioned half-way between the fountain and the hissing sound of the pump that recirculated the water. Mostly, she stared into the water apparently lost in thought. From where I stood, she appeared to be in her seventies, perhaps an ambulatory resident of one of the treatment centers. Or she might have been tired from visiting a grand child in one of the other centers.

She was an attractive woman. Tall, elegant, wearing long pants and a windbreaker, tennis shoes. That first evening I saw her, she took one shoe off and extended her foot down into the water. I enjoyed watching her. She held on to a cedar post supporting an arbor that extended over much of the pond and delicately dipped her toes into the cool water. That moment stuck with me for some reason beyond the physical act.

2.

A few days later, I saw her again. She sat quietly near the same pond. Apparently lost in thought, her eyes looked upwards into tree limbs losing their leaves in the summer heat. She whispered something, but I was too far away to hear. After a few minutes, she stood up and walked back across the campus into the hospice.

I sat down on what I was beginning to consider her bench. The pond was noisy: the gurgling of the water spilling over the rock fountain, the wheezing of the pump. From time to time one of the many white-tailed doves that drank from the pond would stand nearby and lower its head down to the pond to drink. From where I sat I could see the reflection of the trees, the sky, birds on the still surface of the water.

3.

When I taught again the next night and walked out onto the quadrangle, she was already there. I sat down on a bench on the other side of her pond and pretended to read from a book of poems. She walked around the pond and stood behind me.

"What are you almost reading?" she asked.

I looked up at her. "Almost?"

"You've been watching me."

"Yeats."

"I love Yeats. Why have you been watching me?"

She had a soft voice, but not weak. The voice I had thought she would have. "I don't know," I said. "I teach poetry at the school two nights a week. It's a form of therapy for the substance abuse patients. And I walk out here afterwards. I happened to see you."

"Lost," she said. "We are all lost here. In one way or another. It's beautiful, but it isn't real. Why do you watch me?"

I almost laughed. This is what I would have expected of her, a kind of odd flirtatiousness, a directness hinted at by that toe she had dipped into the water.

"Because you're beautiful," I said.

She laughed. "Perhaps. You've read Stevens? 'Sunday Morning'? The part about the ripe fruit needing to fall? If I am beautiful, then that's the reason."

And this is how I had thought she would talk, moving from one thought to another, dropping poetry into the conversation.

"What's your name?" I asked.

"That doesn't matter. I'm dying," she said. "Throat cancer. Too many cigarettes over too many years. Do you know that Yeats poem about the fisherman?"

"Yes."

"You remember, he says 'Before I am old I shall have written him one poem maybe as cold and passionate as the dawn." That's what I want."

4.

I didn't see her again at the center. The term ended and the Substance Abuse Center gave up on poetry. But I think of her often and see her standing there stretching her foot down to the pond and quoting Stevens or Yeats. I never learned her name but she was right. That doesn't matter.

Looking For the Thicket

It is June 6, 2006, D-Day, but I am not thinking about that day when so many soldiers stormed the beaches at Normandy to begin the offensive that would, some time later, end the second of the world wars. I am, instead, walking down a small trail in the middle of what the Indians who once lived here called the Big Woods and the Anglo settlers from Georgia, the Carolinas, Tennessee called the Big Thicket. I have the thicket to myself today. No other cars are parked along the road. Only a hundred yards into the thicket, the trail curves around a giant Loblolly Pine and I almost step on a copperhead water moccasin lying in a small patch of sunlight that has made its way through the first and second canopies. In the Thicket they call them covers, not canopies. The upper cover is the tall trees, long-leaf pine, loblollies, American elms, giant magnolias, bald cypress, beech, water tupelo; the lower cover, smaller trees--wax myrtles, titi, black cherries and more; the third, an uncatalogable collection of small shrubs that would take a whole book to list. I watch the snake for a few minutes, then slowly walk closer to take a picture. I snap the lens when I am about six feet away and the copperhead, hearing the click, slowly turns back upon itself and slides over a maple root, its head passing its tail as it moves off into a titi stand.

What I am thinking about is a different battle. Back in 1927, the year Lindbergh flew *the Spirit of St. Louis* across the Atlantic, the first group of people who lived in the Thicket tried to get 400,000 acres of the land (out of the original 3,500,000 acres of the Thicket) declared a national park. They were not well organized, though, and the lumber interests managed to sidetrack the legislation. The next effort began in the late 30s and was inching toward resolution when the second world war diverted attention from what has been called the "biological crossroads of the United States" and the "American Ark."

Continuing down the trail in the Turkey Creek Area of the Big Thicket National Preserve, I come to a slough that spills over from Village Creek. The Thicket is in the middle of a drought now and the sloughs are little more than baked mud, but the cypress trees, one giant with a trunk diameter close to 9 feet, continue to cool the area in spite of 90+ degree temperature. There are other trees in the dry slough, water myrtle, magnolias, tupelo, but the dominant feature is the cypress stand and some knees that rise five and six feet into the air. From where I sit on the trail, I can see three different kinds of ferns, a small growth of blackberries, most still red, Muscatine vines climbing into some of the trees.

There are no flowers today. The dogwoods and wild azaleas have passed their blooming stage and the more than 25 different species of orchids that grow in the Thicket have had a bad year because of the drought. I'll come back in the spring to see the Thicket in bloom.

If there is a public hero in the whole Big Thicket National Preserve saga, that hero was U.S. Senator Ralph Yarborough. He was brought up in Liberty, Texas, on the opposite fringe of the Thicket from where I grew up. A liberal (and proud of it), populist Democrat, Yarborough proposed a 185,000 acre national park that would include a central area of the thicket located in Hardin County. Supreme Court Justice William O. Douglas visited the Thicket with him and with local legend Lance Rosier, a private citizen who did more to save the Thicket than anyone else. Douglas was struck, as I am today, by the biological diversity he saw. More than 300 species of trees, 3 of the 4 carnivorous plants in the Americas, ferns and mushrooms and hundreds of varieties of wildflowers grow in the Thicket and there are palmetto fields and plants that normally grow only in deserts. The Thicket has soil surfaces from ten different ecological niches and plants that grow normally in the Appalachians, in the desert, in the Florida Everglades, in the Great Plains and elsewhere. It was the summer stopover of the passenger pigeons, buffalo grazed in its plains areas, black bears and jaguars and panthers lived there. Its most famous *possible* resident is the ivory-billed woodpecker, a woodpecker which, from tail to head, measured 23 inches at full maturity. They lived in the long-leaf pine in the Thicket years ago, nesting in the heartwood, but it is doubtful that any survive today. You move along this trail in the Turkey Creek area from sloughs and swamps to arid desert land, past creeks with pure white sand bars, past various kinds of woodland that belong thousands of miles apart, even though the hike is only seven miles long.

I am walking it alone today, packing in my water and cameras, traveling light. I am thinking about the things I see and about Ralph

Yarborough, one of my heroes when I was growing up. He fought the good fight for the Thicket, but shortly after he managed to get the Senate to pass a Big Thicket National Park bill, he was defeated in the Democratic Primary by Lloyd Bentsen and all of us who wanted the Thicket protected almost gave up. Bentsen, though, to everyone's surprise, became a champion of that same piece of legislation.

As I drove out, earlier that morning, some drifts of fog passing over the highway, I could see immediately, without even knowing the history, who the enemy was. In some places I passed grove after grove, mile after mile, of slash pine. These were planted forests, flat-tops, each grove with trees all approximately the same height. Then a different grove, the trees all of a sameness, almost clones, but ten feet higher than the last grove. In the Thicket they say that any bird, squirrel, animal that wants to live in those groves had better pack in its own food and water. The lumber companies clear-cut the area years ago. Clear cutting is a great sin—the lumbering corollary to strip mining. What the companies did was bulldoze the whole area, toppling trees, draining sloughs, diverting the streams. Destroying the land down to three feet below the surface. As Frances Abernathy, author of *Tales of the Big Thicket* has said, the companies consider anything other than a straight tall pine to be nothing more than a weed in their gardens. See the giant white oak over there, its trunk 18 feet around? A weed, pluck it out. See the beaver pond over there? The one with the orchids along the bank? You see, the spot over there where the otters are swimming? Yes. Bulldoze it. Fill it in. You can't grow pines there, only those big old cypress weeds and the magnolias.

There was once a giant oak tree back in the Thicket called the Witness Tree. No tree in the Thicket was larger or older. In the late 1960s, someone, no one knows who, drilled twelve holes deep into its trunk and filled the holes with poison, then capped the holes with wooden corks. The remaining stump of the tree is twelve feet high. What happened to the Witness Tree, what happened to other trees in the Thicket was a form of guerrilla warfare. The dead were the animals who lived there, the trees that were old when even before the Indians first came to the land, the innumerable creeks and sloughs that have vanished from the land.

And the enemy worked with and not, specifically, for the lumber companies. They have names: U.S. Congressman John Dowdy from

Lufkin who fought the idea of preservation for years before being convicted of bribery and U.S. Congressman Charles O. Wilson who had a last minute conversion when the lumber companies began to realize that they were losing their base of community support. When the House of Representatives finally passed a Big Thicket bill setting aside an area not to exceed 85,500 acres (at Wilson's insistence—large parts of the Thicket were in his District and there is an unwritten congressional rule that any congressman can veto any bill affecting his district) and the Senate passed a companion bill with 100,000 acres to be set aside (they added the Big Sandy-Village Creek corridor to the House bill), Wilson managed to keep the House from agreeing to even form a joint committee to iron out the differences. So the Bill that passed, after six decades, and was signed by Gerald Ford was for a park made up of each ecosystem, but separated by private land. A "String of Pearls" spread over the 3,500,000 acres that had once been a solid thicket. The importance of the Big Sandy-Village Creek area is that it would have been a bottom-land corridor, the "string" connecting the "pearls." Some people now consider Wilson a hero for his activity after the lumber companies changed their minds about clear cutting the rest of the Thicket. Without him, though, much more could have been saved and much earlier.

What I see today, hiking through the Thicket, is beautiful; some of the tree are U.S. record trees for size and age. What I do not see on this trip are the great numbers of wild animals that used to live here. I am fortunate, when I walk toward a beaver slide, in a different section of the Thicket, to actually see a beaver in the water. Mostly they are out late in the day after the preserve has been closed to visitors. I see a dozen or so armadillos, but they are latecomers to the place, having migrated here from Mexico in the latter part of the 19th century or even later. When my great-great-great grandparents moved into the Thicket in the 1840s, no armadillos lived there.

Along the beaver pond I see tracks that must be turkey tracks. The wild turkeys vanished from the Thicket in the 1940s but are being restocked by the U.S. Forest Service. The Forest Service also plans to restock the Thicket with black bears. The last one in the Thicket was killed by a relative of mine in the early 1930s. My great-great-grandfather's brother, Ben Hooks, killed three black bears in one day back in the 1890s. That's something I'm not proud of and am not ashamed of. He was a true woodsman and knew the Thicket better than almost anyone else. It did not occur to him that the area would ever need saving.

I have come to the Thicket this time to look for two places that I have never seen, but have read about. The first is Kaiser's Burn-Out. In 1865, the Confederate Army searched in the Big Thicket for Jayhawkers, people like my ancestors who had left Georgia in the 1840s and, when the Civil War started, did not want to fight against the Union. They were followers of General/President of Texas/Senator Sam Houston who had given up his career trying to keep Texas out of the Confederacy. Because they could not find the Collinses, Hookses, Overstreets and others back in the Thicket, Captain Kaiser and his men set the woods afire. No one knows today if any of the Jayhawkers died, but old timers who live in the Thicket and pass on the stories claim that no woods grew back on that portion of the land for generations after the fire.

The other place I am looking for is a small creek called Bad Luck Creek. It is reportedly near Honey Island and Doeskin Pond, but it is unmarked on the maps and has vanished in the drought. Perhaps, though, it had already vanished because the big bulldozers had filled it in and it is now covered with uniform acreage of farmed pine trees. No one I met in the area could tell me. At any rate, I can find neither the burn-out nor the creek. It is possible that they are still there.

In the mid-60s, the artist Michael Frary went into the thicket with Lance Rosier and painted dozens of water colors and did charcoal sketches. Two of these are of Bad Luck Creek.

By the time congress finally got around to passing legislation to create the park, everyone realized that National Park designation was a misnomer. Instead, what they were dealing with was a unique series of biological ecosystems. Nowhere else in the world do so many natural systems come together in such a relatively small area. So, the string of pearls did not become a national park. It became, instead, the Big Thicket National Preserve, the first piece of the American landscape protected simply because of its biological diversity. That biodiversity has also been recognized by UNESCO which made it the first North American part of its Man and the Biosphere Reserves system.

What matters, though, as I walk alone through the Thicket this Thursday is not the politics. The lumber companies came around and began donating bay gall acreage and creek corridors between the preserve areas, perhaps for public relations purposes, but that does not matter to either the State or the Forest Service; and individuals who owned vast tracts of the Thicket have also donated some of their land or left it through their wills to the Park Service. Among the donations was the Big Sandy-Village Creek corridor that environmentalists had long felt was necessary to keep the Thicket natural. Far from shrinking, the Thicket is beginning to grow again. What matters is that down on Village Creek I can see a Bald Eagle roosting on a cypress tree that climbs 120 feet out of the creek bottom, that I have seen a beaver swimming in a natural pond created by himself and his family, that I saw an alligator swim in the sloughs again and that, when I stop walking and listen, I can hear a pileated woodpecker, can hear squirrels running through the trees, can hear a thousand insects (yes, I carried repellant into the Thicket) and that, seven miles deep in the Thicket, I cannot hear a single car.

A Day In the Thicket

Mountain Lions and Other Fauna

Friday morning. Planning to take a ten-mile hike back into the Turkey Creek Unit of the Big Thicket National Preserve and shorter walks in other areas, I got up early and, laden with camera, telephoto, wide-angle and macro lenses, plus a SLIK tripod, drove north on US 69 from Beaumont to Kountze, Texas. After a quick breakfast, I headed north a few miles to the Big Thicket Information Center and got there before the sun rose. The park ranger, according to the sign, would not arrive until 9 a.m., but the hiking trails opened at 6 a.m. and would remain open until 11 p.m. "No Camping in Turkey Creek," one sign said. But I saw another, more important, sign:

WATCH FOR MOUNTAIN LIONS AND FERAL HOGS!

People who have lived and grown up in the Big Thicket area would never call them "mountain lions." Those big cats have always been panthers or "painters" and always will be to people named Hooks and Collins and Overstreet—those people who moved into the Big Thicket area not too long after the Alabama and Coushatta Indians moved in. All of them have heard panthers scream late at night and all have talked about how those big cats sound just like a woman screaming. But, since the 1970s when the Big Thicket National Preserve was carved out of large chunks of what remained of the original old growth wilderness, the U.S. Forest Service has taken over and mountain lions they have become even though there is not a mountain anywhere closer than 500 - 600 miles.

Recently, though, two "mountain lions" are alleged to have been spotted back on Big Sandy Creek, just past Turkey Creek, and rangers say they have seen tracks along the muddy banks of both creeks. No one has mentioned spotting "scat," but perhaps the cats have strong constitutions and have waited until they got out of the Turkey Creek Unit to produce specimens. I suspect "scat" has become such an "in" word among environmentalists that someone would have reported the sight or smell of "cat scat" had it existed.

That feral, tusked hogs have been seen does not surprise me. When my great-great- grandfather and the same number of greats grandmother Hooks migrated from Georgia to the thicket in the late 1850s or early 1860s, probably to avoid being drafted into the Confederacy though there is no written record of that, they had pushed into the thicket driving both cows and hogs. So had the Collinses and the Overstreets and the other early settlers. Some of those hogs, over the intervening decades, had escaped and gone feral. It's natural that some would still be around.

So, when I stepped out from the trailhead, I was a little bit spooked. The beginning of that clearly marked path leads through slope forest with loblolly pines, giant magnolia trees, beeches, black cherry, hickory, long leaf pine, black walnut and a smaller cover of ironwood, bay holly and, in the wetter places, water tupelo and giant cypress trees. Not more than a few yards into the thicket, I spotted disturbed earth: pine needles rooted up, the top layer of dark brown dirt turned over. This was, I thought, a sure sign of hogs. Mountain lions would have come to the thicket, if they actually had, because, I assumed, of the hogs. Mountain lions eat hogs. And, if hogs were near the trail, mountain lions were probably not too far away.

I was no longer certain I still wanted to do this thing I had traveled more than 300 miles just to do. That's how I felt less than a dozen yards into the woods that Friday. I was the only person there. The sun had not risen enough to shed good light through the cover. I had spotted sign, yes, even what I had assumed was scat, of hogs. I was very much tempted to turn back and wait for more people to show up. I'm glad I didn't.

That Friday, in the four different units of the Big Thicket National Preserve I walked through, not one other person showed up all day. I suppose the beginning of the school year and the temperatures that had shot up into the low hundreds were the primary reasons for my solitude.

When you walk alone in the thicket, everything seems extremely quiet except for the bugs that would like to feast on you. They buzz in, swirl around you and, if you are wearing a thick coating of repellant, as I was, fly on off to find a sweeter smelling breakfast. That's all I heard at first—bugs. Although the sun had already risen, the thick cover in this part of the thicket kept the trail fairly dark until almost 8 a.m. and it was still too dark on the trail to set up the camera. I stopped walking for a moment and sat down to listen. For a few seconds, everything seemed quiet...again, with the notable exception of a few bugs. I put my camera bag and two quarts of water down on the trail and looked warily around. This was, I believe, the first time I had ever been hesitant about walking into the thicket.

Did I say the thicket is extremely quiet? I spoke much too soon. The thicket is never quiet. When you sit very still and pay attention, you can hear the steady fall of leaves and pine needles. It sounds like a light sprinkle of rain. As the sun climbed higher into the tall trees that morning, two squirrels raced around the trunk of a long-leaf pine and everywhere they jumped I saw something fall to the ground: leaves, pieces of bark, cones. The thicket was noisy; I just hadn't noticed it until I stopped and listened.

About half a mile down the trail, I rested on a bank beside a large cypress slough. The sun had finally risen high enough that light, in particle-filled streams, slanted between the trees to hit the still water. I attached the camera to the tripod and mounted the wide-angle zoom lens on my old Pentax K1000. The water was dark, slimy, a thick layer of lichen covering most of it. A log moved. I watched more closely. What I saw was one of a growing number of the alligators that have repopulated parts of the thicket since they became a protected species several years ago. They live in the cypress sloughs and baygalls and all along Big Sandy and Village Creeks.

I heard woodpeckers drilling into the trunks of trees. Some woodpecker species are forever silent in the Big Thicket now, most notably the Ivory-Billed, a huge woodpecker which once nested in the old forest long-leaf pines that have been harvested by the logging companies. Even the pileated woodpecker's numbers have been severely depleted and their distinctive sound is rarely heard these days. What I could hear was squirrels running around and around and, off in the distance, the cawing of black crows. Everywhere, I heard the steady dropping of leaves onto the lush forest floor. Nearby some animal made a strange noise as it pushed through the thousands of pine needles and the thicker leaves of the magnolia trees. And I froze. Hogs, I thought, rooting through the ground matting.

Picture this: I am standing on a low ridge that circles a dank slough filled with alligators. Okay...at least one alligator I have seen, perhaps more that I have not spotted. The water is dark brown from the tannin of the pine trees and a thick coat of algae covers most of it. I can see hundreds of cypress knees, some more than five feet tall. Some animal I cannot see is rooting in the leaves behind me. I have read only this morning a sign warning that feral hogs are in this unit of the Big Thicket. What I did was to look quickly for a magnolia tree nearby or two of any kind of tree close enough together or with low enough limbs that I could shinny up. Young magnolia trees are easiest to climb because of their almost evenly-spaced branches, the old ones that grow more than a hundred feet high in the thicket don't have branches until you climb twenty or thirty feet up, so what I really wanted to find was a young one. The last time I checked hogs could not climb trees.

When I spotted a likely magnolia, branches drooping near the ground, I took off running and jumped into the lower limbs. The young tree almost bent over with my weight as I climbed five feet very quickly. I looked around and saw nothing on the thicket's floor but leaves, my camera and tripod and water bottles. I was not quite as stupid as that preemptive race to safety made me appear. I knew, intellectually, that if a hog had caught sight of me, that hog would probably have run the other direction...unless I got between a sow and her litter. And litters do not swim around in foul-smelling cypress sloughs populated by alligators. I knew I had made a mistake. I was the only person in this section of the thicket. I had read a notice telling me that feral hogs and mountain lions had been spotted in this unit. I had heard a rooting sound and had over-reacted. I climbed down from the tree.

As I walked back to my camera, I made a lot of noise. Should there have been what I truly knew was not around, that non-existent thing would run from me if it knew I was here. When I got back to the camera and the slough, I listened again and heard the same scuffling noise. This time, feeling foolish, I investigated. I saw a small animal pushing through a matting of pine needles. Hardly anything but his ears was visible and an armored back curved like a narrow turtle's. What had frightened the scat out of me that early Friday morning was a small, absolutely harmless armadillo. They are not native to the thicket, but migrated from Mexico back in the latter part of the 19th century, after my ancestors had already migrated in from Georgia.

Spotting this small animal delighted me, not only because I had a simple, safe explanation for the rooting noises and the turned up earth, but because I had not seen an armadillo in the wild for years. No, they are not threatened, they are not rare, they are so common that I can hardly drive along the roadways of Texas without seeing them as road kill. William Cronon explains it very well in an essay he called "The Trouble with Wilderness":

> [Remember]: the moment on a sandstone ledge, your boots damp with the morning dew while you take in the rich smell of the pines, and the small red fox—or maybe for you it was a raccoon or a coyote or a deer—that suddenly ambles across your path, stopping for a long moment to gaze in your direction with cautious indifference before continuing on its way...and you will know as well as I do that you were in the presence of something irreducibly nonhuman, something profoundly Other than yourself. Wilderness is made of that, too. (*New York Times Magazine*, 1995)

For me, that morning, a small armadillo had been my Other and had, somehow, made me shrink from an environment that has been a part of my family for generations. That day, I had ignored the advice of General Patton and had taken too much counsel of my fears. I watched the armadillo for a while, snapped some photos of the slough and the 'gator and walked on down the trail.

Small Carnivores

Every relatively wild area has its carnivores—predators both small and large. The Big Thicket used to boast a variety of big and small predatory animals: jaguars, panthers, black bears, wild cats, alligators, various raptors, bob cats, wolves, foxes, coyotes and many more. Today, the larger of those animals have vanished from the area. Hunters did some of the damage. But most of the damage came from the destruction of habitat and the extremely wasteful practice of clearcutting. People did not, for example, set out to wipe out the ivory-billed woodpeckers with shotguns and rifles. Instead, they cut down the longleaf pines and, since the ivory-billed woodpecker nested only in the rotten heartwood of the oldest pines, drove them away or into extinction. Some birds and animals may have been wiped out by over-hunting, but the loss of habitat would have driven them out of the thicket anyway.

Decades ago, one of my great uncles is supposed to have killed the last black bear known to have existed in the thicket. I'm not proud of that, but for him it was natural. He and his family had led groups of hunters from all over the country into the thicket for years for just that purpose. Not to eradicate all the bears, but to hunt and kill the ones they could track. Mountain lions have been spotted again in the thicket only recently. There are occasional, not very reliable, reports of a black bear being spotted, and people claim to have seen red wolves every once in a while though most people suspect the animal was actually a fox or coyote.

That Friday I spent in the Big Thicket I did manage to see hundreds, perhaps thousands, of carnivores. After I had spotted that small, harmless armadillo near a cypress slough about half a mile into the Turkey Creek Unit, I lost my last nervous twitch and walked deeper and deeper into the preserve. Six or seven miles back from the highway, some acres of fairly wild savannah grow dazzling arrays of wildflowers in the spring and some flowers at all times. I walked down a trail that led past towering pines and magnolias and beech trees, around sloughs and baygalls, and out into not quite dry, almost always slightly damp, meadow lands.

The savannahs in the thicket are caused by a change in soil conditions from the sandy, loamy dirt that produces the slope forests to an impermeable high-clay content soil. The hills begin to vanish and the land is low and almost flat—a shallow bowl that catches and retains water except during times of severe drought. This year, the normal fifty inches of rain in the Thicket has been cut in half, but the ground remains slightly wet though water no longer pools in small cavities. The impermeability of the soil not only retains rainwater during wet seasons, but also prevents water from seeping up during drier times. The result is a soil that is low in nutrients, but one that supports a sparse community of pine trees, a variety of ferns and mosses, and four of the five types of carnivorous plants known to exist in the United States.

I walked back into this part of the thicket to photograph two of those carnivorous plant species: pitcher plants and sundews. They are radically different in appearance, but have the same survival strategies: a thick, sweet-smelling aroma that attracts bugs. Pitcher plants attract insects to crawl into a conical bowl that has hairy spikes pointing down so that they cannot climb back up. Sundews have a sticky substance that traps the bugs as leaves roll over them. Neither is dangerous to anything much larger than the last knuckle of your little finger.

When I headed downhill, leaving all of my gear except a jar of water and my camera and tripod under a black gum tree, the trail was clear and flat. I walked around a burned out area (burned by the forest service—absolutely essential since we have fewer and fewer forest fires these days and the forests need those fires) and then looked out onto the savannah. It was almost breathtaking after the darkness of the slope forests and the cypress sloughs. Flowers everywhere! I can't name them all but there were wild daisies, black-eyed Susans, cinnamon ferns and Christmas ferns and other flowers sprinkled into a land of high grasses. This was not even the best time of year for the flowers. In the spring, hundreds of varieties, including some species of orchids bloom in the thicket.

At this time of the year, though, I did spot huge patches of pitcher plants looking much like smiling jokers with the overleaf that shades the opening to what must be a chamber of horrors for flies and other insects. They filled much of the savannah, growing around the shoots of newly planted long leaf pines. Most were pale yellow, shot through with green veins, but many had a thin undercoating of red. They stand erect waiting for gnats, flies, other insects to be attracted to their perfume and fly down into the spiny inner surface where they are trapped and digested.

What I have always loved about this area is its almost total transformation, in just a few steps, from the darkness of the double canopy to a bright sunshiny meadow scene. I sat on the ground and drank in the bright sunshine and flowers for what seemed like hours. I did not doze off though I did nod a little. I listened closely and could still hear sounds from the nearby trees and, not often, a few bugs zipping by.

But what I enjoyed most was the bright sunlight after I stepped out of the heavy, deep woods. I was reminded of Dylan Thomas singing in "Fern Hill": "It was all / Shining. It was Adam and maiden / The sky gathered again / And the sun grew round that very day." But this Eden was a barely visible charnel house and I got the impression that the pitcher plants were munching away, bugs rotting down in the bell of the flower, small corpses not even spat out. But, of course, these carnivorous plants do not chew, do not swallow, do not spit, and had I not known they were carnivores, none of this imagery would have conflicted with Thomas's words. This was not the "Little Shop of Horrors," only one manifestation of how nature adapts, how plants survive in areas hostile to them.

Finally, I sat down among the pitcher plants and opened one of the overhanging leaves to look inside. The sides sloped toward the bottom of the bell with tiny spines pointing down to keep its food from climbing back up and out. The one I looked into had not made a recent capture, but at the bottom of the cone, I could see the remains of the same kinds of bugs that had been buzzing around me all day.

I Get Lost in the Woods

I keep trying to find some reason for it other than stupidity, but when I was walking around in the beaver slide area of the Big Sandy Unit of the Big Thicket, I managed to get lost in one of the most inhospitable areas. Today, I am more embarrassed by that than anything else, including my having run from a small armadillo earlier in the morning.

I parked my car along the highway, gathered my camera equipment and a quart of water, and walked down an old road to a spot where a rather generously wide trail bent into the undergrowth. I slipped off the road and onto the trail, clinking and clanking a bit from the tripod slung over my shoulder and the camera bag and water I carried on my back. Usually I don't pack so much equipment, but that day I was interested primarily in getting some good landscape shots in parts of the Thicket I had not visited in years. I also knew that the Forest Service had marked the trails. There were, though, some things I did not know.

About a hundred yards down the trail, I walked across a wooden bridge over the creek. A group of boys from a Boy Scout troop had built the bridge as their Eagle Scout final project. I knew that because the troop's number was carved into the first plank. As I noted before, the Big Thicket has much wilderness, but of that, much of that is no longer pristine.

When I slipped off the road and onto the Beaver Slide trail, everything grew quiet. The soil was almost black, and close to the creek, slippery lichens grew over every downed limb. This is not swamp land, but it is close. The whole time I spent in that area of the thicket, I did not for one moment walk in an area that admitted sunlight, other than an occasional splash when the wind higher up blew a branch to the side for a moment. Nothing on the ground except the lichens and various toadstools and mushrooms gave off color other than shades of brown. The major exception occurred when the small trail opened onto one of the beaver ponds. I am calling them beaver ponds because the ponds grew behind dams made years ago by an active beaver population; some, but not very many, beaver remain in the area and I did not see any on this trip. What is left is the result of their activity many years ago: dams packed down with dirt, dank ponds that attract some water birds and alligators, a maze of ponds that I can walk around. And a sudden blinding of sunlight over the dark water. Some kind of water fowl flew by, bright white in sunlight, a flash of light, an exclamation point that disappeared around a bend in the creek. I suspect it was a white heron, but cannot be certain.

The major populations here seemed to be spiders and alligators, frogs and crayfish—tall mud chimneys excavated by the crayfish stick up to a foot above the ground in places—mosquitoes and wasps. I did not see a single animal or the tracks of any. But I did use the tripod to brush the trail ahead of me and knock down countless spider webs to keep the spiders off. It is oppressive country. Still, hot, humid. But it has its own beauty: constant drips of water, unexpected brightnesses, clusters of trailing vines. I kept my eyes open, watching for water moccasins, the other populous species in this area. And I saw them. Not everywhere, no, but around and about the trails. Slate gray cottonmouths, coiled, mouths open and white, that kind of white that reminds you of Melville's disquisition on the whiteness of the whale—a kind of passive-aggressive sign of evil and death, some old malevolence that has been replaced for most of us by newer urban darknesses.

But I have strayed from the path. That day I wandered through the area I got rather hopelessly lost. I walked around five separate ponds, saw two or three alligators, several snakes, dozens of mud chimneys, hundreds of spiders, a few water birds, no beavers, no people. I did see the archeological evidence of people—some beer cans and trash at one spot along the trail. I should probably have been outraged at this sign of desecration, but instead I thought about the creek parties we used to have in the Thicket when I was in high school and was mildly amused that the tradition continued. When I stopped to listen, I could hear only the hum of mosquitoes and the dripping of water, the plopping sound a turtle makes as it drops off a bobbing limb in the water to swim underwater. I must have taken fifty or sixty pictures when I finally decided to pack up and head home.

I walked back down the trail, retracing my steps. I came to a pond with bright white sand along the bank. I came to a second pond, the bank undercut by the water, crumbling as I stepped close to the water's edge, a motionless alligator sitting like an old log on the bank. I brushed through a spider's web, the long yellow legs of the banana spider visible as it fell below me. I jumped over a small puddle of water and walked around yet another pond. After an hour of walking, I came back to the white sands of the first pond and realized that I was circling an area maybe a mile in circumference and a few miles into the thicket from the highway. I sat quietly and listened, but could not hear anything that pointed the way back to the highway. No, I don't mean I was listening for a particular wild sound I might have heard earlier, but for a car horn, tires squealing, a reassuring sound of uncivil civilization. I heard nothing but that constant sound of mosquitoes.

What had happened was that the summer had been so hot no one had bothered to walk very deeply into the thicket and the trail turning out of the Beaver Slide area had been overgrown. The thicket fills in such trails quickly. A branch might have fallen, a single limb drooped down, or maybe my eyes were just not sharp enough to see the mouth of the small trail back to the road.

I headed off down the ponds trail again and once again wound up at the same spot. I was tired and hot, my shirt drenched with sweat. I drank the last of the water from my jug and decided that circling the ponds on the small trail was simply not working. Several things passed through my mind at that time: stories of people lost in the thicket never to be found again, my grandmother singing songs about the "poor little babies lost in the woods," Hansel and Gretel and their accursed bread crumbs, black bears adopting lost children who had strayed too deeply into the Thicket. All flights of fancy and there was really not much in the long run to worry about. I had signed in at the trailhead and my Cherokee was still parked, unless someone had stolen it, at the spot on the highway where the trail began. Someone would have noticed and, after dark, or maybe the next morning, people would have been shouting for me. You don't necessarily think of those things, though, when you are sitting near an algae-covered pond, lost, and looking at water moccasins, alligators and large yellow-jointed spiders.

One of the reasons people get lost in the woods, even rather deep thicket, is that they keep moving and don't do a lot of thinking. That's what I had been doing: circling on the same trails around the same ponds as if moving were a solution in and of itself. I finally stopped in place for several minutes and created mental pictures of some of the areas I had photographed earlier and managed to remember the first time on this trail that I had set up my tripod. I had snapped a quick shot of the first of the ponds I had seen. It's not a particularly good picture, but I could still see the composition in my mind. In the middle of the small pond, the blackened stump of an ancient cypress tree rises up, jagged shards of the trunk stretch about five feet into the air, and it is surrounded by two- to three-foot high cypress knees. I remembered a beech tree leaning out at about a 45 degree angle from the bank on the side of the pond closest to the entry trail.

I started to walk around the ponds again. I came upon that first pond from the wrong side, but I could see the old cypress stump and, when I walked across the dam and positioned myself at the right place, I saw the same beech tree leaning out over the water. I turned my back to the pond and walked about fifteen feet, pushed back a branch, and was on the main trail. Not much of a story, granted, but enough excitement for the day. I got back into the Cherokee and drove north to the Alabama-Coushatta Reservation to have a few glasses of beer and a couple of buffalo burgers.

Going Home

While I rested from my own stupidity in getting lost, I decided to do something I had not done in years: take the Alabama-Coushatta's train ride into the Big Thicket. It isn't much of a ride, maybe a one-mile circle on narrow-gauge track, but someone else would be responsible for getting me from Point A and back to point A in a circle, a circle that is intentional instead of accidental. In exchange for hopping a ride (at $1.75) I got to shake along on a wooden bench and listen to the "chief" crack wisely about Anglos.

It's only fair. I did the same thing with the train years ago in the first part of one of my first published poems:

My own country is thicket, a thousand
kinds of trees, alligator sloughs with titi
stands and water moccasins, Alabama-Coushatta

Indians chuff-chuffing tourists on trains
through ancient stands of laurels, beeches,
and pines so tall you never see the tops.

This time, I did not even listen as the train chuff-chuffed through the Thicket and circled back. I was, quite simply, too tired. Being lost, even for only a couple of hours, in the thicket is enervating and all I wanted to do was doze off. I munched on the sandwich of barbequed buffalo that I had lugged along with me as the day began to come to an end. The sunset was spectacular, more varieties of red, yellow and lavender than I had ever seen as the sun dropped behind tall pines to the west and striped the ground around me with the shadows of other pines. There is more, of course, to a great sunset than its beauty. Keats did not have it completely right. Truth is beauty, but beauty often hides rather ugly facts. Southeast Texas has some of the most colorful sunsets I have ever seen because of its polluting industries: the paper mills of the Thicket area, the refineries just east between Beaumont and Port Arthur. I didn't care about that all that much that Friday afternoon. I was tired and enjoyed eating over-cooked barbequed buffalo and French fries as I slugged down a cold beer, rode on a tourist gimmick train, and watched the night begin its descent.

The Big Thicket and the Death of James Byrd, Jr.

It is not easy to love a place so much and at the same time realize that it is haunted by a past and present that is violent and incredibly racist. Sometimes the violence and the racism come together as they did a few years ago with the murder of James Byrd, Jr., a 49-year old African American living in Jasper, Texas. Jasper is a few miles past Kountze, Texas, and Kountz is, arguably, the central town of the Big Thicket. Kountze is where an editor named Archer Fullingham and his *Kountze News* worked for years with Senator Ralph Yarborough and others to carve the "string of pearls"—87,000 acres of the remaining thicket that had once spread from northern Florida to Texas—into the Big Thicket National Preserve. I was in the Thicket hiking and camping just a week and a half ago.

You see, that's the land that, when I think back on my past, to the years and people who formed what I am, that's the land that is home. It's the land that produced me and that produced James Byrd and that also produced three men who could look at James Byrd and not see a man, three men who could only see a thing that they called a "nigger." Three men who beat up James Byrd and tied him to the back bumper of their truck and dragged him for miles...dragged him until parts of his body broke off the main trunk...dragged him until his head separated from his body and lay beside the road.

Jasper, Texas, just north of Kountze, Texas, which is only 30 miles from Beaumont, is nestled among tall pine trees and is a beautiful little town. It's people say, "We're not like that. We're not like Vidor, Texas," which is an even shorter distance east of Beaumont and where William Samples first integrated public housing only a few years ago and was later gunned down in Beaumont, Texas, my home town...not by white men, but by African Americans.

All of that land, filled with rivers and creeks, with snakes and wild cats, with alligators and wild hogs and even wilder dogs, all of that land is beautiful and is often dangerous. If you walk through it and are not careful, you can be bitten by snakes, attacked by dogs and hogs. If you swim in Village Creek or the Big Sandy or the Neches River, the waterways that keep the thicket alive, you can drown from the numerous snags and whirlpools that appear. But the most dangerous thing about the Big Thicket, as with other wild areas, is the people.

Lawrence Russell Brewer, Shawn Allen Berry and John William King all grew up in the Big Thicket. They gave James Byrd a ride in their pickup. They tied him to the bumper after beating him and they dragged him down a road until long after he was already dead. What James Byrd did to cause these three "men" to kill him was to exist and to live in Jasper, Texas.

I love the Big Thicket. I go hiking in the area whenever I can. Earlier in that year of the murder, I walked down the sundew trail, near the Turkey Creek Unit of the Big Thicket National Preserve, and I saw wild orchids growing. As I walked through that savannah area of the thicket, I saw pitcher plants and sundews, two of the wild carnivorous plants that thrive in the thicket. They use their colorful appearance and sweet odor to attract small insects and, then, when the insects make the mistake of walking on the petals of the sundew or moving inside the open bowl of the pitcher plant, they are lost. They cannot get out of the pitcher plant with its spines pointing down to the liquid at the bottom of its horn-like bowl to dissolve them and provide nutrients for the flower. The sundew closes its petals over them. And they die. But the plants are dispassionate in their killing. They stand and wait for the small insects to land on them.

There was nothing dispassionate about the three killers of James Byrd. They picked him up as he walked along the road and offered him a ride. And they killed him. They enjoyed killing him. Sport. Don't imagine that the people who used to hang African American men, women and children, set fire to crosses in their yards, attack them if they tried to vote, kept them down, down, down, ever acted dispassionately. Racism is always passionate.

I do not think I will be able to hike in the Big Thicket for some time without thinking about James Byrd and about Lawrence Russell Brewer, Shawn Allen Berry and John William King. King's father said, "It hurts me deeply to know that a boy I raised and considered to be the most loved boy I knew could take a life." I doubt that his son thought he was taking a "human" life. Racism and hatred do not work that way. When I walk in the thicket again, as I will, and see carnivorous plants growing among beautiful wild orchids, I will think of these people and other people I grew up with when the South was still legally Jim Crow and when no one would have protested the sport of killing men who happened to have a different skin color.

That things are improving cannot be doubted. Thirty years ago, we would not have heard the cries of a whole community in denial. Instead, we would have heard bitter jokes and Lawrence Russell Brewer, Shawn Allen Berry and John William King would be treated in some places as if they were heroes. For this murder, they were charged and convicted. That's an improvement, though not one that will help James Byrd, Jr. I do not sum up the recent schoolyard murders in various locations in the country, the murder of a black man in the Big Thicket, the constant violence and hatred we are faced with on an almost daily basis as the collapse of civilization, but I do come close to despair at these things.

The first time I hiked deep into the thicket after the murder, I picked an orchid. I carried the flower to Village Creek and threw it into the slick brown water in memory of James Byrd and as a token that things are getting better in the aggregate, though that is of little consequence to him or to his family.

Jasper: on the Trail of James Byrd, Jr.

I am somewhat nervous as I pass the city limits sign for Jasper, Texas. A year and a week ago (July 7, 1998) three men had offered James Byrd, Jr., a ride home. They had tied him to the bunker of their pickup and dragged him alive down Huff Creek Road until parts of his body littered the roadside. Poems I have written about the Big Thicket and about the death of James Byrd, Jr., were featured a few years ago as "Big Thicket Requiem: an Elegy in Six Parts for James Byrd, Jr.," in *Palo Alto Review* . The magazine included several photographs I had taken of the Thicket as well as a few I am coming to Jasper to take just for that issue.

I stop just inside the city limits (Jasper Pop. 7,109) when I see a small roadside monument and get out to snap the first quick photo. It is not a memorial to James Byrd, Jr.; instead it is a celebratory monument to Jasper's being named a "Texas Main Street City" a few years ago. It's a nice little monument: flowers and a small plaque with an advertisement for the landscape company that maintains it.

But this is not what I have come to Jasper to see though it remains, in some ways, perhaps ironically, very fitting.

I turn off U.S. 290 toward the heart of the town: a classic small town square. In the block at the center of the square sits a stucco court house surrounded by dogwood and other trees. This is the center of town and the sidewalks across the four streets that make up the square are filled with small shops. In the center of the square, the first of the three men who murdered James Byrd, Jr., has already been sentenced to death. The second is on trial while I am in Jasper, but the trial is recessed today. On one quarter of the square is the county jail, the place where Lawrence Russell Brewer, Shawn Allen Berry and John William King were first held after their arrest for the murder. I take pictures of both locations with only a few people around on this hot day. I have not yet spoken to a single person in Jasper.

What I want is a photo of James Byrd's grave site, the monument, what I know will be hundreds of flowers. But I do not know where he is buried. I walk a few blocks away from the courthouse and see a sign directing me to the Jasper Public Library. It's a nice building, small and not enough books inside as is common with most isolated small town libraries. I walk around a bit inside, mostly enjoying the air conditioning, but also because libraries always attract me, especially libraries in small towns. Yes, they do not have enough books and, yes, they try to appeal to the tastes of their own publics. So, most do have the current best sellers. But most of the librarians in small towns like Jasper feel a real sense of responsibility to their communities and make a strong effort to maintain the community's own sense of history.

I introduce myself to the reference librarian and tell her what I am looking for and why: that *Palo Alto Review* is running a long poem I have written about the Big Thicket and the death of James Byrd, Jr. She takes me immediately to a special newspaper file the library is maintaining on James Byrd's murder and the public reaction to it. It's a fine collection and includes various WEB sites. Public libraries in small towns like Jasper often can and do provide internet access for their citizens and Jasper Public Library has printed off several of the more prominent pages dealing with the James Byrd, Jr., murder. I take a number of notes and then go back to the reference desk.

The librarian gets out a map of Jasper and directs me to the site of the Jasper City Cemetery where the murder victim was buried. "It's easiest to go down Main Street, but he's buried near the Crockett Street side of the cemetery do turn around the cemetery when you stop and enter from that side. You can't miss it." I should not be amazed at how friendly and helpful the librarians are. I am a librarian myself and the librarians who work for me give the same kind of helpful and friendly service to the students at St. Mary's University. But I cannot help but think that after the frenzy of the last year, the people of Jasper, including the librarians, must be getting tired of all the attention. It helps, I suspect, that I am not a newspaper or television reporter, only a librarian/poet doing something that I hope will be a worthwhile memorial to James Byrd, Jr.

I drive down Main Street past the courthouse until I get to the cemetery. Cemeteries always depress me and I suspect that's true of most people. Row after row of tombstones at the Jasper City Cemetery, thousands of flowers in blossom, a celebration of the dead since the middle of the 19th century. I read the names on the stones: Horn, Byrd, Hooks, Roberts. Except for the name "Byrd," these are the names of my ancestors. They settled in the Thicket and in the Jasper area in the mid-19th century and have lived, loved and died here ever since. I walk to the center of the Crockett side of the cemetery and am almost blinded by the burnished-silver coffin lid that gives the name of James Byrd, Jr., and his birth and death dates. My God, I think, this is a coffin that demands attention. I look down onto it and see blue sky and clouds reflected. At night, I am certain I could see the stars. I suspect this is precisely what the family and NBA basketball player Dennis Rodman, who donated most of the money needed, wanted: something that when a person looks in reflects back the territory surrounding him.

Look directly down from above and you see yourself, the sky framing your head. For we are all, I think, buried there with James Byrd, Jr., our innocence, our belief that racism has vanished from the country. And the shining silver also gives hope that maybe this is the last time, that maybe we have finally learned something. I am sure the people of Jasper have.

I drive back down to the library. One of the clippings I had read indicated that the Byrd family had planted a tree last week, on the anniversary of James Byrd, Jr.'s, death at the site of a future park. But I walk past the library and down the street to city hall. I ask the city clerk how to find the site of the future park, but she does not know. She calls over the head of parks for Jasper and he tries to show me where it is on the map, then says, "Hell, I'll drive you over there." We get in a city truck and drive through Jasper again, this time into a neighborhood lived in mostly by black residents of the town. On Burch Street at Black Street, I see an empty block. A bulldozer is parked with no one around it. I walk up onto the elevated land and manage to find a small, enclosed area. A young oak tree, filled with leaves, grows there. A handwritten sign says, "This tree was planted on June 7, 1999 in Memory of James Byrd, Jr. (May 2, 1949 - June 7, 1998) 'Love Never Fails.'"

I learn later, at the library, that a similar tree had been planted in Israel to demonstrate solidarity against the kind of hate crimes that took the life of James Byrd, Jr., and that Israelies remain so very much aware of.

With the final snapshot of the tree and the sign, the photos of the grave, and the courthouse square, I have finished what I came to Jasper to do. I find myself liking Jasper, Texas, a lot. The people have been friendly and helpful though most must be really tired by now of writers descending upon them. I stop by to thank the librarians and donate a copy of *Deep Thicket and Still Waters*, my collection of poems about the Big Thicket and about the killing of James Byrd, Jr., then drive farther south to Beaumont to spend the evening with my mother and sister before heading back to San Antonio the next day.

Driving Through Milwaukee

Last night I dreamed the world was coming to an end and I was in Milwaukee. The war was over. I drove home on interstates with numbers so low they had to be south and west, not north and central. I was young, the age when I came home from a different war and crashed with Ann and Marilyn and Sonya on Rio Grande Street in Austin in 1969, three years before I would meet and marry Susan, eight years before my son was born.

But I was talking about Milwaukee, a place I've never been, and how the world was coming to an end. I drove on a freeway past row houses and old factories, perhaps a brewery, this being Milwaukee and all, and even in my dreams I have to build from something if I'm in a place I've never been before. On a sharp, clear day, the sun bouncing off metal roofs, I drive an interstate that does not exist through a city I've never seen and I am surrounded by old friends, some of whom I've never met.

The bumper sticker on the car ahead says MY KID CAN BEAT UP YOUR HONOR STUDENT and vanishes with its car heading down an off ramp to somewhere...or not. I am almost always happy when I'm driving even when I have no destination in mind, just wheeling off down a road that, with luck, I've never driven before. Like driving through Milwaukee on this particular afternoon when nothing happens except a few old friends appear, vanish, reappear.

I am in the house on Rio Grande Street and I am in Milwaukee and I am sitting in an old chair. Linda, who never lived there, is on the floor, her cheek against my knee, her long dark hair flows down my leg as I drive past an exit sign that says Khe Sanh—20Km. We were never lovers, Linda and I, for some reason neither of us has ever figured out, but it's right somehow that she is here in Milwaukee as the world is coming to an end.

My friend Don is in the passenger seat as we drive past a baseball stadium, circle it, watch a batter hit the ball and a fielder catch it in the web of his glove, hear the sharp crack of the meat of the bat, the lighter slap of the ball hitting leather. Don and I landed in Chu Lai together and he was the best man at my wedding and now we are driving through Milwaukee and Linda is sitting on my lap, shifting gears as I push in the clutch.

When you're driving through Milwaukee, even if you've never been there, and the sun gives everything a bright golden aura and the world is coming to an end, you need close friends and, aside from Don, all my close friends have been women. When I exit by a park and turn the car down a dirt road that does not exist in a greenbelt in a big city I have never seen before, Linda is sitting by my side, Linda, who married four times, three to history professors.

Twenty-two years ago, at a graduate student party, someone announced to everyone there that Linda wanted to go to bed with me and, at that moment, I told the group that Susan and I were getting married in August. Linda died of thoracic cancer ten years ago, but she's here in Milwaukee and we talk about why we never went to bed together, yet loved each other. At two of her weddings, I gave her away and, I suppose, spent most of our time together doing so.

Dreaming through Milwaukee and thinking of the past I drive by some kind of flour mill, a strange building tall and not very wide or long, old red bricks and huge letters on the side, PIONEER FLOUR, perhaps. I am not married and I have no children and the top is down and there is no smog, no unpleasant smell as I drive through the city which is called Milwaukee but contains parts of Houston and Austin and San Antonio, the cities that bred me, grew me up, and spat me out so many years ago.

I question this dream from time to time, almost wake up, wonder why I am in Milwaukee and why I am driving and whether there is some destination and why the world is coming to an end, but the dream doesn't answer. We drive across a river, Linda and I, and go to the Corcoran Gallery, transported from across the street from the White House to the middle of a park in Wisconsin and we are out of the car and sitting on the floor, beneath my legs glass brick and green light shining through, and a band at the front, a band that no longer exists, a band called Love Cry Want is playing sitar music accompanied by a panoply of instruments from Thailand and Burma. A big man in dreadlocks moans into a microphone as the walls move in and out and the green light hits my face. Linda hands me a small cup with sugary liquid stuff and I drink a little and pass the cup to a guy sitting to my left and watch the walls come to life, breathing in the same rhythm as the music.

I am dreamdriving through Milwaukee and I am on something or perhaps something else and the city begins to shimmer, fracturing into a thousand brilliant colors I have never seen before, not even in this dream where Milwaukee becomes something more than Laverne and Shirley ever thought it could be and Linda and I are making love, not moving, just the smooth vibrations of the car rolling over the freeways of the city and the world is coming to an end.

On Rejection and Acceptance, All Wrapped Up With The Beats

March 3, 1999: the kind of day I would love to be outside. The Dutch Iris are blooming, water lilies are beginning to poke large buds up through the water, the Lady Banks roses are already blooming and the Lantana has gone wild in a riot of purple and orange blossoms. Me? I'm inside, working, weeding through fifty manuscripts, rejecting poet after poet.

I am reminded of that Dilbert cartoon: Dilbert asks Dogbert How's the publishing business going? The answer: "I get to reject dozens of authors every day. I call them untalented dolts and they thank me for it." "Eventually you actually have to publish something," Dilbert says. "Yeh, well, that's the conventional wisdom," responds Dogbert.

Well, I do publish other people's poems and, sometimes, stories and essays, but unlike Dogbert, I hate Rejection Day and usually make it on a Wednesday afternoon when I am always exhausted from attending too many meetings and from teaching. I finished *A Farewell to Arms* with my students today and talked a bit about the first Beats, Jack and Lucien and William and Allen and the murder of Dave Kammer and just kind of free associated on them for a while and for no apparent reason. Maybe a reason: I don't like my students thinking of "writing periods" as being somehow distinct from each other. Hemingway and Faulkner were still writing when "Howl" and *On the Road* were published. William Cullen Bryant was writing when Emerson penned "Nature" and Thoreau, *Walden*, and Whitman, the first edition of *Leaves of Grass*. There is nothing really separate about them in terms of time "period," though the aesthetic was different.

So, I yammered on and on: Lucien and Dave met at the San Remo after Jack and Lucien were unable to get a job on a ship and went back to have a few drinks. Dave was deeply in love with Lucien who considered himself nothing but straight (not like Neal who could and did swing both ways), but Dave persisted, kept coming on to Lucien (Lucien, the most beautiful of all the Beats) until, finally, irrevocably, Lucien pulled out his Boy Scout knife and stabbed Dave three times in the heart then stripped him and dumped him into the river. After that, he went back to William Burrough's apartment and told him what had happened. Burroughs, living with Joan Vollmer, whom he had not quite married, advised Lucien to get a good lawyer.

But Lucien went to Kerouac's place first and banged on the door. Kerouac left Edie's bed and took a long walk with the new murderer. On the walk, Lucien threw the knife down a grate into a sewer and buried Dave's glasses (and, oh, could that be a true symbol from life, not literature?). Jack Kerouac, never sure of his own sexuality, loved Neal and Allen, even physically at one point. Neal loved everyone physically, perhaps even the cars he delighted in. And so on I yammered. I quoted from "Howl," talked about the Beats and about the Lost Generation on this last day in class, a class session that was supposed to be dedicated to Ernest Hemingway.

And I came back to my office to reject poems. Some of them are by very good poets, but you can't publish all of even the very good poets who submit to your magazine and it's depressing to have to reject good poems and good writers. I know, from the other side of the desk, that I get depressed when my own work is rejected, but it's good to remember, too, that editors cannot accept every even good poem that is sent to them. I know the question that must follow: Then why do I read so much dreck in even the most revered magazines? I don't know. *A chacun son gout.* Beats me. Different editors, different readers, different strokes.

Of course, I accepted some poems, some writers. Some readers would undoubtedly disagree with me on whom I should and should not have accepted, rejected. I don't really care. They can always start their own magazine or press. I do not mean that to be hostile; most of those reading this quite probably have already done that. After all, that's precisely what Lawrence Ferlinghetti did with City Lights. That's what anyone, including me, who has ever started a magazine or press, in print or on the WEB, has done.

I am rambling, mostly because all these rejections have become depressing. I now receive 25 - 30 book-length manuscripts each month, and in those manuscripts of 50 - 115 pages, I sometimes find a poem or two that I think really sings, but rarely a whole book's worth. Good poets for the most part and, for the most part, not yet ready for a book. I always reject those book manuscripts, but sometimes invite the poets to submit their very best stuff to my magazine.

Kerouac spent years working on *The Town and the City* before he found his publisher and then more years before the publication of *On the Road.* After that, he had no problem in publishing any of his work, not even the prose that is pretty bad. William Carlos Williams pushed Ginsberg's poems for years before Allen found a publisher. *Rejection, rejection, rejection.* And we are all, all of us who reject and accept poems, wrong every day. We are, on some day like this, going to miss discovering a great poem because of our own sensibilities. I regret that, but can't do anything about it.

When I finish rejecting and accepting poems (not rejecting poets) today, I will go home and muck the pond. I will tear loose the overgrowth of parrotsfeather to give the lilies more room, will trim back the plumbago that did not freeze back over what we call a winter here in San Antonio, Texas, and I will sit in my backyard on one of the Adirondack chairs and read *On the Road* again before class on Friday or, maybe, read a poem or two, not for acceptance or rejection, but just to take pleasure in the words.

More Than a Simple Game

I don't often go back to Beaumont, Texas, for any reason except to visit my mother. But I decided to go back for my 40th high school reunion. The reasons are not complex: I wanted to see what everyone looked like and to meet some of the people who had actually been friends of mine in high school: Robert Husband, Herman Weber and Douglas Nielson, Ruth Willard, Cynthia Marshall, Sandra Wainwright, Helen Sample and Marian Holland. Friday night, the four of us who are male met at Herman's house to play a game of poker and reminiscence. I lost at poker, mostly, I suspect, because my face tends to reveal things that in poker should not be revealed. I admit, too, that I was not terribly comfortable. Perhaps it's vanity, but they all seemed older than they should have seemed: gray hair or bald, all three much too overweight. My hair is still predominantly brown and I weigh less than I weighed in high school.

We've all been okay, even relatively prosperous. Only Robert and I have had major illnesses and surgeries: my kidney cancer seven years ago, my heart and brain surgery more recently, and his brain tumor from which he continues to have narcolepsy. Douglas was, at one time, head of computing for Tenneco and Herman is Human Resources manager for the City of Pasadena. None of us is wealthy, merely middle-class, but considering where we started from we're doing very well.

We played for three hours and talked about the past then I told them I'd see them at the reunion party the next night. I was the second to leave—Robert's wife had dropped by to pick him up and I wanted to get to sleep early because I was playing golf the next morning with some of the jocks left over from high school.

I guess this begins the point of this journal entry and, if it sounds somewhat angry, I regret that. It needs to be told, if at all, in present tense, so I'm shifting tense and, if you are reading this, bear with me over those little literary rules. This isn't fiction, it's truth as I see it.

The Beaumont Country Club takes up property along the Neches River across from one of the units of the Big Thicket National Preserve. I write about the Thicket a lot, but this is not about that mostly wild place. The BCC (that's what the Tee markers label it) is also across the street from the largest cemetery in Beaumont, many of my ancestors and relatives lie there waiting for whatever. A marker is there for my father though his body was never found when his ship sank. My grandmother is there and my mother already has a small piece of the real estate purchased for her future use.

None of the people I knew across the street from the BCC would ever have been allowed to get out of their cars in the parking lot. And me? I'm playing golf there today.

Sometimes, we behave irrationally and I suspect my attitude during much of October 6 fits into that category. Thinking about it now, I confess that I would probably not invite me to join the BCC either. I am not their kind of people.

I took a few practice swings, addressed the ball, set my feet and absolutely smashed the ball close to 300 yards and straight down the middle of the fairway. Please be aware that my normal handicap is 20 and that means my average score is 20 over par and that means my average score on a course that is a par 72 should be about 92. I am sitting about 62 yards from the first green after drilling the little white ball in the best tee-shot I have ever made in my life. None of the other players (a pick up group—it's a little wet and others from the reunion group didn't show) hits nearly as well. One slices his ball into the 18th fairway, another hits about 180 yards but keeps it in the fairway and the third hooks left but has a clean shot in. I chip to about 2 feet from the cup and no one else is on the green in regulation. After a short putt, I birdie the first hole. Two of the other players bogey the hole and one double bogeys. Summation: after the first hole, I have 3 strokes, two others have 5 and the last has 6. I win the hole. I suspect a couple of the players believe I have sandbagged them on my handicap (claimed a handicap much higher than I should have), but that isn't true; I merely played out of my ass.

I am not going to give a play by play of the whole game and, no, I did not break par for the day, but my playing partner and I win all three parts of the Nassau and I win the largest number of holes and have low score even without having to use my handicap. I hit an 84 which is pretty good for someone who's only been playing for three years and who didn't start until he was in his fifties. Oh, hell, I will mention one other hole: the par 3 17th. It's an island green 154 yards from the tee box and is stunningly beautiful. Two of the guys go in the water, another hits the sand on the front and my ball (hit with a smooth, relaxed 7-iron) hits the pin and bounces to a stop about a yard away. As I said, I think everyone believes I have lied about my handicap. What actually happened?

On every hole I play I am pissed off, but this is a rather cold angry feeling, and it is not the fault of the guys I am playing with. If you put a canoe into the river at the country club and paddle about a mile north, you can, if you know the way, paddle right into the back yard of my mother's house. You have to fight your way through a Cypress slough, but you can do it. Every hole on the course and all of the ponds are named for someone who has, without knowing them, hurt my family. They own the factories that gave my mother asbestosis; they own the refineries my father worked in and they own the sulfur company that killed him when his poorly-maintained ship sank. They did not do this intentionally; it was merely a by-product of doing business. And they would have excluded him and my mother, not personally but for economic and social reasons, from association.

Do not get me wrong, my parents never applied for and could not have afforded to be members if accepted. But country clubs throughout the south are symbols of wealth, prestige and entitlement and even had my parents been able to pay the dues and applied for membership, they would not have been accepted. I should not have been as angry as I was and, as angry as I was, I should not have played well. But I am and I did.

I do not go home after the game. Instead I drive west into the more prestigious area of the city: big houses, well-maintained estates. When I get to Gladys Street, I turn left and drive straight down to Magnolia Boulevard. At first I am driving through very rich neighborhoods, but then I cross IH-10 and things change dramatically. I am in a predominantly black neighborhood that was predominantly black forty years ago. Gladys Street and Magnolia Avenue are the heart beat of what the folks at the country club, when they feel they are alone and do not have to observe the proprieties, continue to call "Niggertown." It is also the heart of the music that has sprung from the area. People like Johnny and Edgar Winter used to go down to Gladys Street and listen to jazz and blues. I do not know, but suspect that Janis used to go there. Mance Lipscomb played there.

Music and the church: the heart of the community. I sit, parked for a while, right at the corner and look at the rubble of the old places that used to be there. The churches have mostly fallen down, no corner stores exist there anymore, no one is walking on the street. It's all being urban-renewed out of existence. I turn onto Magnolia and drive a few blocks north, turn down Elm Street to Cable and look at a vacant lot. That's the house I was born in. Next door to it was Charley Stidham's house. He was my best friend until we moved from there into the federal project called Multimax.

Charley's not at the reunion. He's long dead now, in a plane crash, but he and I were inseparable for five or six years. His father was a true asshole, an old Wobbly, who drank and was rarely there. When he was, Charley always wanted him to leave. I confess that I felt somewhat the same way about my own father and his ever-present belt. These were the days when he was a heavy drinker and wasn't very tolerant of noisy children. By the year 2000, we will call it child abuse, but he came through somehow, thanks primarily to a preacher who helped him get off the booze.

I drive down Junker Road, alongside the woods, until I get to Gulf Street. Across Gulf Street is a football stadium and a little bit to the left of it is the Babe Didricksen Zaharias Museum. The Babe was another Beaumonter who made good. I've been driving and thinking and getting madder and madder and no one has really done a damned thing to me. It's the past coming back. Leeching in like it's supposed to do at times like this. I drive back home and take a nap.

When I wake up, I get dressed. The invitation says "dressy casual" and I correctly interpret that to mean sport coat, nice polished shoes, dressy shirt and tie. How nice to guess the correct definition! And then…I almost don't go. I get in my rented car and drive out to the thicket. I pull off on a dirt road (much like one Mary Karr describes in *Cherry*) and drive down to Village Creek. It's getting dark early and the whole weekend has been gray with intermittent rain. I just sit in the car, motor turned off and listen to the creek. It's a magic place though I don't think Karr much appreciated it when she was there. Wading in the creek almost always makes me feel good and just sitting there listening to it convinces me to go back to the Beaumont Country Club. There are people I have still not seen; people I really sort of want to see.

I walk into the country club and see dozens of "old" people, people I went to high school with. But I also see Ruth Willard. Ruth is a wonderful and loving human being and still looks younger than almost everyone else there. We hug and talk for about 30 minutes before Sandy Wainwright shows up. Sandy wasn't as good a friend back in high school, but I'm delighted to see her. Somehow we all get separated and then the whole group is pulled together…for a prayer! One of our graduates is now a Baptist preacher and he leads the whole damned group in prayer. Prayer's good, don't get me wrong, though I do it less and less often as the years pass, but this prayer keeps on and on and he prays for things I don't approve of. I catch Ruth's eye from across the prayer circle and she winks. We are both laughing at the whole thing. Finally it ends and I wander away.

The next person I bump into is Cynthia Marshall (all of the names here are real though some of the women have changed theirs since high school, but these are the names I remember them by and are the names I'm using). Cynthia, Amy Hill, and I all teach at the college level. Like Ruth, Cynthia is wonderful and always brings out the best in me. And like Ruth she's stayed amazingly young over the years. We get interrupted in our conversation by the guy who organized the evening. He's up on the dais to introduce a speaker, Congressman Rex SomethingorOther (this isn't to protect his identity, I simply can't remember his last name) who drones on for at least half an hour. He's a right-wing asshole--I know this because Cynthia said so and, when he finally brings his speech up to the 60s and begins proclaiming about how awful the best years of my life were (since we were caught by a left-wing cabal and threw dirt upon our parents' fine images—I believe he was actually thinking about those people who were in high school there a few years after us, but if the shoe fits and other cliches).

I suggest to Cynthia that we stage a protest and march out. She's says "Right on! Let the sanctimonious son of a bitch try to figure out whether or not we decided to run out into the bushes and make love not war." People near us do murmur a bit as we stand up from the front table and march out.

I guess, finally, this is another story about the women in my life and not really a story about golf after all. It's about Ruth and Cynthia mostly and I love and honor them to this day. I am, at last, glad that I went, happy to have come together with old friends, some of whom are still friends. I wish Charley could have been there, but am glad Ruth and Sandy and Cynthia were. What is it about the women in my life? They turn me around, move me in new directions. Not in the traditional, narrow sense of hearth and home, but even women I have not seen in years seem to know just how to...well, I can't explain it.

About the Author

H. Palmer Hall's previous books and chapbooks include *The Librarian in the University* (1990), *A Measured Response*(1993), *From the Periphery: poems and essays* (1994), *Deep Thicket & Still Waters* (1999), *Reflections on Writing, Publishing & Other Things*(2003) and *To Wake Again*(2005). His poems, essays and stories have appeared in many literary reviews, including *North American Review, Ascent, The Texas Review, Borderlands, The Texas Observer, The Florida Review, Palo Alto Review* and many others and have appeared in various anthologies. He is a Vietnam veteran and, also, a veteran of many protest marches against American participation in that war. He is the editor of Pecan Grove Press and director of the Louis J. Blume Library at St. Mary's University.